Refugees: A Very Short Introduction

VERY SHORT INTRODUCTIONS are for anyone wanting a stimulating and accessible way into a new subject. They are written by experts, and have been translated into more than 45 different languages.

The series began in 1995, and now covers a wide variety of topics in every discipline. The VSI library currently contains over 650 volumes—a Very Short Introduction to everything from Psychology and Philosophy of Science to American History and Relativity—and continues to grow in every subject area.

Very Short Introductions available now:

Available soon:

For more information visit our website

www.oup.com/vsi/

Gil Loescher

REFUGEES

A Very Short Introduction

OXFORD
UNIVERSITY PRESS

OXFORD
UNIVERSITY PRESS

Great Clarendon Street, Oxford, OX2 6DP,
United Kingdom

Oxford University Press is a department of the University of Oxford.
It furthers the University's objective of excellence in research, scholarship,
and education by publishing worldwide. Oxford is a registered trade mark of
Oxford University Press in the UK and in certain other countries

Published in the United States of America by Oxford University Press
198 Madison Avenue, New York, NY 10016, United States of America

British Library Cataloguing in Publication Data
Data available

Library of Congress Control Number: 2020948744

ISBN 978-0-19-881178-7

Printed and bound by
CPI Group (UK) Ltd, Croydon, CR0 4YY

Links to third party websites are provided by Oxford in good faith and
for information only. Oxford disclaims any responsibility for the materials
contained in any third party website referenced in this work.

Contents

List of illustrations

Foreword

This is a special book. After a career spanning some forty years, after hundreds of meetings with refugees and those on the front lines of refugee responses around the globe, and after writing some of the most influential and transformative works in the discipline of refugee and forced migration studies, this is Gil Loescher's last book.

Gil Loescher died on 28 April 2020. He was in the final stages of preparing the manuscript for this book, which he considered to be one of his most important.

Before you read this book, it is important to know who wrote it and why it was so important to him.

Gil was a gentle giant of refugee studies. His writings on refugees and world politics were pioneering and endure as a cornerstone for the discipline. For example, his 1993 book, *Beyond Charity: International Cooperation and the Global Refugee Crisis*, remains a critical reference for all work that asks how the international community can be mobilized to ensure protection and lasting solutions with and for refugees.

His work inspired generations of researchers, policymakers, and practitioners engaged with refugee responses.

But more important than his work was who he was as a person. Gil was humble, empathetic, thoughtful, curious, and kind. Gil cared about people, and he was more interested in hearing about the work and ideas of others than promoting his own.

It was especially important for him to understand the views and experiences of those closest to the refugee experience. Gil often said that he never wanted to be an 'armchair academic'. In the acknowledgments to his 2001 book, *The UNHCR and World Politics: A Perilous Path*, he wrote: 'Over the last two decades, I have visited numerous refugee camps in Africa, Asia, and Central America as well as refugee holding and detention centres in Europe and North America . . . [and] interviewed or spoken with hundreds of officials, human rights and humanitarian aid agency workers, researchers, refugees, and asylum-seekers on every continent.' This was a defining feature of Gil's work.

And he was always moved and inspired by the courage and resilience of refugees. In Chapter 5, Gil tells the story of visiting Thailand in 2006, just three years after being badly injured in the bombing of the UN Headquarters in Baghdad. Gil was in a wheelchair, and the only way he could visit the rehabilitation centre for refugees with disabilities in one remote refugee camp on the border between Thailand and Myanmar was for a group of six refugees, themselves amputees, to carry him, in his chair, up a steep and slippery path. It remained for him one of the most powerful examples of the strength and determination of refugees.

But Gil was deeply troubled by world events in recent years, especially how the rise of populist and exclusionary politics and misinformation contributed to a breakdown in international cooperation and collective action. This was most painfully on display in 2015 when the European Union, one of the most affluent and powerful political communities on the planet, failed to cooperate to provide an effective and rights-based response to the claims of some 1 million asylum seekers—constituting just 0.02 per cent of Europe's population.

As his family wrote in their tribute to him after he died: 'The global refugee exodus and rise of the far right in recent years troubled Gil greatly and added to a deterioration in his health. In recent years he suffered from heart failure and his hearing and eyesight were failing him. As his immediate surroundings gradually faded with his sensory loss, his four grandchildren were still a great joy to him, but he has worried about the world in which they are growing up.'

Gil's hope was that this book would be read by people wanting to understand the complexities of refugee movements and to take informed positions on the issue for themselves.

I spent three days with Gil in February 2020 working through the manuscript for this book, discussing ideas, and helping with corrections and revisions. We had collaborated on several projects since 2001, and our work together over those three days was just like old times. It was the last time I saw Gil, and I will forever cherish that time together. He was a dear and exceptional friend.

When Gil died with the manuscript unfinished, his family asked me to make the final revisions to the book. Even though I saw it through the publication process, these are Gil's words—his clearly considered and honestly deliberated words. These are the words of a great scholar and greater human being who cared deeply about these issues and devoted himself to understanding and explaining them to anyone who wanted to listen.

Gil wanted you to read this book. And no one could have said it better than Gil.

James Milner
Ottawa, Canada

List of acronyms

CRRC	Cambridge Refugee Resettlement Campaign
CRRF	Comprehensive Refugee Response Framework
DFID	Department for International Development, UK
DP	displaced person
DRC	Democratic Republic of the Congo
ExCom	Executive Committee of the Programme of the United Nations High Commissioner for Refugees
FGM	female genital mutilation
GCR	Global Compact on Refugees
GRN	Global Refugee-led Network
HIAS	Hebrew Immigrant Aid Society
ICRC	International Committee of the Red Cross
IDP	internally displaced person
ILO	International Labour Organization
IOM	International Organization for Migration
IRC	International Rescue Committee
IRO	International Refugee Organization
IS	Islamic State
LGBTI	lesbian, gay, bisexual, transgender, and intersexual
MSF	Médecins sans Frontières
NGO	non-governmental organization
UNDP	United Nations Development Programme
UNHCR	Office of the United Nations High Commissioner for Refugees

UNRRA	United Nations Relief and Rehabilitation Agency
UNRWA	United Nations Relief and Works Agency for Palestinian Refugees
USAID	US Agency for International Development
WRY	World Refugee Year

Refugees

Chapter 1

Who are refugees and other forced migrants?

We are now witnessing the highest levels of forced displacement on recent record. By the end of 2019, there were 79.5 million people in the world who were displaced for a great variety of reasons. Most are refugees, asylum seekers, and internally displaced persons who are fleeing violence, conflict, religious or ethnic discrimination, and persecution. In recent years, a growing number of people have been forced to flee due to the increased frequency and intensity of natural disasters and environmental crises such as earthquakes, hurricanes, floods, drought, and other disasters that destroy peoples' homes and livelihoods. At the same time, growing numbers of people are fleeing failing states which can no longer provide the means of survival such as physical safety, jobs, food, or medical care for their citizens. In addition, greater numbers of migrants are seeking a better and often safer life for themselves and their families.

Refugee and migrant stories

Why do all these people flee or leave their home countries? Who receives international protection and assistance and who doesn't? Here are some fictional stories to start answering these questions.

When war broke out in Syria in 2011 **Mohammad and Fatima** were engaged to be married and lived in Homs Province. Their town was attacked by Syrian forces and they fled to southern Syria. Soon afterwards, the Syrian secret services arrested Mohammad, his father who had spoken out against the Assad regime, and two of his brothers in law and his cousin. They were taken to Homs prison where they were beaten and tortured for several months.

After his release from prison, the security forces continued to harass Mohammad and he soon fled across the border to Lebanon where he was eventually reunited with Fatima. In Lebanon they were treated horribly by their landlord who cheated them and threatened them with eviction. They also felt unsafe because the local population taunted and attacked them.

After three years, Mohammad and Fatima were selected to be resettled to Canada. With the support of a community sponsor group in Canada, they were able to improve their English skills and understanding of Canadian society. After being in Canada for one year, they opened a restaurant serving traditional Syrian cuisine. The restaurant has proved to be a great success, and now employs five Canadians.

Ayesha is a Rohingya Muslim who has lived all her life in northern Rakhine state in Myanmar (formerly Burma). Although Rohingya Muslims have resided in the country for more than a century, Burmese government policy has rendered them stateless and has systematically crushed the cultural, religious, and ethnic aspirations of the Rohingya people and denied them citizenship and their basic rights. They are the largest stateless population in the world.

One evening in late August 2017, Ayesha was eating dinner with her sisters-in-law in their village of Tami in Myanmar's Buthidaung Township when Burmese army troops attacked the hamlet. Soldiers forcibly entered their home and made the women move into an adjoining room. Ayesha recounts that the soldiers ripped her baby from her arms and kicked him 'like a football'. The solders then stripped the women naked, held a knife to their throats, and gang-raped them.

After the soldiers left, Ayesha picked up her baby and fled with her sisters-in-law to neighbouring Bangladesh. During their dangerous journey to safety the two sisters-in-law who had been raped died. Ayesha now lives as a refugee in an overcrowded camp near Cox's Bazaar in Bangladesh.

When **Tigish** was 18 years old, he left Ethiopia to find work in South Africa in order to send back money to support his family. On his way to South Africa, he spent a month in Kenya and Tanzania but was stopped in Malawi before he reached South Africa. He was arrested by the border police because he had entered the country illegally. For the next eight months, Tigish was imprisoned in Malawi before the International Organization for Migration (IOM) eventually helped him to return home to Ethiopia.

Tigish says he would never migrate irregularly again because he witnessed many of the risks that other irregular migrants faced such as hunger, physical abuse, and even death in some cases. As a migrant, he was not eligible for refugee status, but he could receive assistance from IOM, the Office of the United Nations High Commissioner for Refugees (UNHCR), and other international organizations.

In late 2018, **Arianna** and her husband and two children faced an intolerable and potentially dangerous situation in their home country, Venezuela. For many years the country's leaders had pursued failing political and economic policies which impoverished their people. Hyper-inflation wiped out Arianna's and her husband's savings. The country's economy was in free fall caused by widespread mismanagement and corruption. Severe shortages of food and medicines created record numbers of malnourished children and adults. Thousands died of hunger and untreated diseases. In addition, organized crime and drug trafficking endangered the daily lives of nearly all Venezuelan citizens. Consequently, in recent years over 4 million desperate Venezuelans have fled to nearby countries such as Colombia, Ecuador, Brazil, and further afield in the Caribbean, North America, and Europe in search of safety and a better life.

Arianna and her family were eventually forced to seek safety in Colombia and are now termed 'survival migrants'. Currently they are not eligible for refugee status under the 1951 UN Refugee Convention. However, the UNHCR is providing critical assistance to those Venezuelans in great need who have taken refuge in neighbouring countries. Moreover, they are given protection under the 1984 Cartagena Declaration, which expanded the coverage of the UN Refugee Convention in the early 1980s to those persons fleeing generalized violence and severe human rights violations in South and Central America.

Satina lives on the South Pacific island of Tuvalu. She works on a small plantation that grows coconuts, a main export for the small island. Over the years, the sea level around Tuvalu has continued to rise. Salt water has started to contaminate the soil in the plantation, making crops less and less abundant. Stronger storms have made this problem more acute and have resulted in the loss of more agricultural land. With the loss of her livelihood, Satina finds herself without the means to support herself. She gathers the last of her savings and flees to New Zealand, where she claims asylum. Her claim is rejected because New Zealand does not recognize climate change as grounds for being a refugee. Satina waits in limbo as her case continues to work its way through the New Zealand courts.

Unlike those displaced by war, systemic violence, or persecution, people like Satina who are forcibly displaced from their home country as the result of environmental change are rarely recognized as refugees when they cross borders to seek safety. There are millions of such desperate people across the world. Some estimates predict that there will be 200 million people forced to flee their homes due to climate change by the year 2050.

How are refugees defined?

Refugees, asylum seekers, internally displaced persons—what's the difference? According to the 1951 United Nations Refugee Convention, **refugees** are defined as persons who, 'owing to a well-founded fear of persecution, on the grounds of race, religion, nationality or membership of a social group', find themselves outside their country of origin, and are unable or unwilling to avail themselves of the protection of that country. An **asylum seeker** is someone who has fled her home country and is seeking protection from persecution or conflict in another country as a recognized refugee. States are under international legal obligation to consider claims for asylum and not to immediately return asylum seekers to the country from which they had fled.

In short, persons recognized as refugees are individuals who have fled persecution and conflict in their home country and no longer enjoy the legal protections afforded to citizens of a state. As a consequence, the 1951 Refugee Convention stipulates that refugees should be protected and should have access to national courts, the right to employment and education, and a host of other social, economic, and civil rights on a par with nationals of the host country. In addition, the Convention grants the right of *non-refoulement*: the right not to be involuntarily returned to a country where there exists a risk of persecution. Non-refoulement is now a principle of customary international law. Most importantly, most refugees are entitled to the protection of a UN agency: UNHCR.

In addition to refugees under the protection of UNHCR, there exist more than 5.5 million **Palestinian refugees** housed in over sixty camps spread throughout the Middle East and the Gaza Strip under the authority of a separate UN agency, the UN Relief and Works Agency for Palestinian Refugees (UNRWA). Palestinians in countries where UNRWA works are excluded from UNHCR's mandate and are not covered by the 1951 Refugee Convention because Arab states wanted the issue of Palestinian refugees to be addressed separately. Unlike UNHCR, however, UNRWA has no mandate to protect Palestinian refugees and its main function is to provide assistance to activities in education, healthcare, and public services for Palestinian refugees in Lebanon, Jordan, Syria, the Gaza Strip, and the occupied territories in Israel.

Since UNRWA's founding, the United States has been the organization's largest funder. That changed in 2018 when the Trump administration stopped all funding for the Palestinians, who now face an even bleaker future. Unresolved conflicts and acute unmet needs, particularly in the West Bank, Gaza, and Syria, are creating a major humanitarian crisis. Today some Palestinians are fourth generation refugees and have been in exile since 1948 and still hope for a return to their homeland. Palestinians remain the world's oldest and largest protracted refugee situation.

Over the past seven decades usage of the term 'refugee' has expanded beyond the legal definition of the 1951 Refugee Convention to cover people in diverse situations who need assistance and protection. For example, in 1969 the Organization of African Unity adopted a regional instrument which includes as refugees people fleeing both individual persecution and 'external aggression, internal civil strife, or events seriously disturbing public order' in African countries. In addition, the 1984 Cartagena Declaration covering Central and South American refugees also expands on the 1951 Refugee Convention by including 'persons who have fled their country because their lives, safety or freedom have been threatened by generalized violence, foreign aggression, internal conflicts, massive violation of human rights or other circumstances that have seriously disturbed public order'.

Since the signing of the 1951 Refugee Convention and the establishment of UNHCR, the circumstances that shape displacement have progressively changed. New drivers of displacement such as unchecked gang violence, the widespread availability of lethal weapons, environmental change, natural disasters, and food insecurity are widespread throughout much of the Global South. Consequently, in response to the changing nature and conduct of warfare and growing risks caused by environmental and demographic pressures during recent decades, UNHCR has increased its operational and protection activities from assisting and protecting solely refugees to include stateless populations and internally displaced persons.

In addition, while not recognizing victims of natural disasters, failed states, or endangered migrants as Convention refugees, UNHCR has in recent years also expressed growing concern for these groups of forcibly displaced people. Consequently, UNHCR may now offer assistance to victims of hurricanes, earthquakes, tsunamis, floods, and other natural disasters in many circumstances. As discussed below, this protection was extended in January 2020 when the UN Human Rights Committee stated that the provisions of non-refoulement now extend to people who flee their countries due to 'climate change-induced conditions that violate the right to life'.

Many governments, especially those in the Global North, have strongly resisted this pragmatic expansion of the refugee definition. In Western countries, the definition contained in the 1951 Refugee Convention, with its focus on individuals and on persecution, is used by states when determining if refugees can be admitted to their territory. Governments have a strong interest in keeping the definition of refugees narrow because of the obligations they have to refugees under the Refugee Convention.

If the refugee definition broadens, states are concerned that they will face obligations to a greater number of people. Nevertheless, groups of people at risk of death or grave harm from violence if prematurely returned home are often granted temporary protection. This means that they are not forced home, but they do not enjoy the same rights as recognized refugees.

Unlike refugees, **internally displaced persons** (IDPs) do not cross borders to seek protection and assistance abroad. Despite fearing persecution and violence, they stay within the territory of their home state. While there were some 24 million refugees in the world at the end of 2019, there were more than 45 million IDPs.

IDPs remain under the jurisdiction of their own government, even in cases where government forces or authorities are often the ones responsible for their displacement. State sovereignty prevents the international community from intervening without the permission of the home country, unless the UN Security Council authorizes such action under Chapter VII of the UN Charter. Hence UN agencies and other international actors must seek permission of national authorities and at most play a subsidiary role of supporting government action even in situations where a government has withdrawn its presence from areas of displacement and its citizens are stuck and at risk in conflict zones.

Despite the differences between refugees and IDPs, in recent years the international community has accepted that IDPs are a specific category of international concern. States regularly reaffirm their recognition of an international framework for the protection of IDPs, namely the UN's 1998 'Guiding Principles on Internal Displacement'. Similarly, the adoption in recent years of the Kampala Convention in Africa strengthened cooperation on this issue at the regional level and clarified the rights to which IDPs have access.

While progress has been made in defining the rights of IDPs, ensuring adequate responses to their needs remains a challenge. For more than fifteen years, the UN has used a 'cluster approach' to respond to the needs of IDPs, from education and nutrition to protection and reconstruction. This approach draws on the expertise of ten UN agencies and relies on the ability to coordinate an effective response from a diverse range of actors, all with their own agendas and structures. This has made responses to IDP situations problematic, leading to recent calls for a new approach. In response, the UN Secretary-General announced the establishment of a High-Level Panel on Internal Displacement in 2019. The group is tasked with improving international responses to internal displacement.

There are also more than 4 million **stateless persons** in the world today. These are persons who have lost or are denied their nationality, are without citizenship or other documentation, and have few rights. For stateless people, daily existence can mean discrimination, fear, and exclusion. The lack of nationality traps some in a cycle of poverty, destitution, and life on the fringes of society. They include, for example, the Biharis in Bangladesh, the Muslim populations of Burma/Myanmar, in particular the Rohingya, who reside in or originate from northern Rhakine state and who comprise about one-tenth of the world's stateless population, the Bedouins throughout much of the Middle East, some Kurds in Syria and Iraq, the Roma (gypsies) in Europe, Muslims in Kashmir and in India and in many other stateless populations across the world.

During the 1990s, the dissolution of the former Soviet Union and the Yugoslav Federation caused migrations that left hundreds of thousands of people stateless throughout south-eastern Europe. Over thirty years later, tens of thousands of people in the Balkans and Ukraine remain stateless or at risk of statelessness. In Southeast Asia, Myanmar has denied citizenship to its minority Muslim population—the Rohingyas—for decades and has not even recognized them as a distinct ethnic group. There have been three periods in the last forty years during which the Burmese army and militant Buddhist monks have ruthlessly attacked, murdered, and forcibly expelled the Rohingya population. The UN and many governments have condemned such actions as 'classic ethnic cleansing' and others have called it genocide.

In general, the true scale of the problem of statelessness across the world remains obscure because of a lack of awareness and inconsistent reporting. Few countries have procedures in place for their identification, registration, and documentation of stateless persons. While there exist two UN conventions on statelessness—the 1954 Convention relating to the status of stateless persons and the 1961 Convention on the reduction of statelessness—stateless people experience widespread violation of their human rights. These include lack of documentation, such as birth certificates, non-recognition of the right to reside in the country of their birth, and constant risk of forcible expulsion, discrimination, human trafficking, and gender-based violence. Many also experience limited access to healthcare, education, and property ownership, along with many other restrictions.

How many forced migrants are there?

Together, refugees, asylum seekers, and IDPs are referred to as **forced migrants**. According to UNHCR, there are more refugees and other forced migrants today than at any time in the organization's history. By the end of 2019, some 79.5 million people—1 out of every 97 people on the planet—were victims of forced displacement caused by wars, violence, human rights abuse, and rising tensions over identity with respect to ethnicity, religion, and politics. Of this total, 45.7 million were internally displaced, 26 million were refugees, 4.2 million were asylum seekers, and 4.2 million were stateless. Roughly half of those refugees and asylum seekers are under the age of 18.

While the numbers of refugees and IDPs are alarmingly large, they are not without precedent. For example, at the end of the Second World War, there were more than 60 million refugees in Europe alone, in addition to millions of forcibly displaced people in Asia. Moreover, since a European and worldwide refugee crisis in 2014–15 there has been a dramatic drop in the numbers of asylum seekers and refugees who have arrived in Europe. Finally, it is important to keep in mind that there has been no significant increase in the number of refugees as a proportion of the current total global population of some 7.8 billion people.

According to UNHCR, the vast majority of refugees flee to countries neighbouring their homelands, most of which struggle to meet the needs of their own populations. The largest refugee-hosting states at the end of 2019 were Turkey (3.6 million), Colombia (1.8 million), Pakistan (1.4 million), and Uganda (1.4 million). Refugees are generally hosted in camps or settlements or have taken refuge in urban areas, and large numbers are self-settled among populations in regions where they often share similar ethnic or religious ties. For example, most of the 6.6 million refugees who have fled persecution and war in Syria since conflict broke out there in 2011 have taken refuge in neighbouring Turkey, Jordan, and Lebanon.

In fact, at the end of 2019, 85 per cent of the world's refugees were in the Global South, in low- and middle-income countries that are in the refugee's region of origin. This means that the responsibility of accepting and assisting refugees falls mainly on regional host countries that are already facing challenges in providing for their own citizens. For example, over the span of just a few months in late 2017, more than 700,000 Muslim Rohingya refugees from northern Rhakine state in Myanmar fled to Bangladesh, one of the poorest and most densely populated countries in the world, where they continue to receive protection and assistance today.

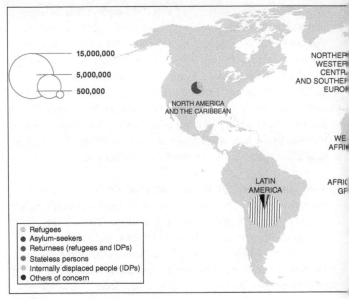

1. **Global distribution of forced migrants, 2017.**

Only a relatively small percentage of the world's displaced have sought asylum and protection in the Global North (Figure 1). Nevertheless, since the 1980s, a significant number of people from the Global South have travelled across dangerous territories and vast deserts and open seas to seek asylum in Europe and North America. Throughout 2014 and 2015, more than a million people fleeing conflict, persecution, and economic and political failure in their home countries attempted to seek safety and asylum in Europe. Large numbers of desperate people made dangerous journeys across the Mediterranean Sea to Greece, Italy, and Spain and trekked onwards to seek asylum in northern European states. Thousands lost their lives when unseaworthy boats crammed with desperate people and having no means of navigation capsized and sank in the sea. While the numbers of people from Libya, Tunisia, and elsewhere seeking refuge in Europe have declined rapidly in

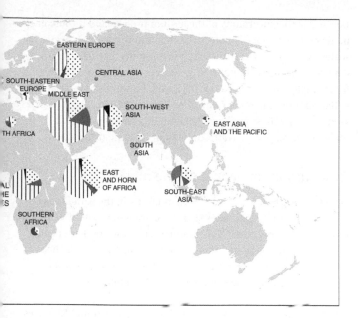

recent years, significant numbers of people still risk their lives crossing the open seas in search of asylum and safety.

The 1948 Universal Declaration of Human Rights guarantees those fleeing persecution the right to request asylum in another country. However, because host states consider immigration and asylum a matter of national sovereignty, asylum practices differ from country to country. The government authorities who review asylum seekers' applications usually determine whether one is a refugee on a case-by-case basis. Asylum seekers will be asked to prove that they were persecuted in their home country and explain why they are afraid to go back. Usually those persons who are found not to qualify for asylum as refugees are either deported to their country of origin or are given a temporary right to remain. UNHCR reported that 4.2 million people were awaiting the results of their request for asylum by the end of 2019.

Because of the uncertainty of the asylum process and its outcome, many people do not even file for asylum but live in the margins of society as undocumented self-settled migrants fearing arrest, deportation, and other punitive measures. In the United States, for example, during the past thirty years, hundreds of thousands of Salvadorans and other Central Americans fearing being denied asylum have self-settled illegally and many feared expulsion under a radically more restrictive Trump administration.

Other groups of people on the move

While there are 79.5 million forced migrants in the world today, the United Nations estimates that there are more than 250 million **international migrants**. This number has grown by 49 per cent since 2000. Although the number of migrants far exceeds those of refugees and other forced migrants, it still only comprises about 3.4 per cent of the world's population of 7.8 billion.

What is the difference between a refugee and a migrant? Refugees have left their country to escape persecution or violence. Most migrants, on the other hand, are moving across borders, and even continents, to improve their livelihoods and to achieve better conditions and prospects for themselves and their families.

Perhaps the most important distinction between the two groups of people on the move is the fact that international law treats these two categories of people differently. The legal distinction between refugees and migrants is based on an understanding of voluntary versus involuntary movement. The international refugee system, based on the 1951 Refugee Convention and the mandate given to UNHCR in 1950, was designed to respond to the needs of people who are understood to have been forced to flee their home country due to a well-founded fear of being persecuted. International migrants, in contrast, are generally understood to have chosen to leave their home country to seek opportunities in other countries.

Migrants are not protected by a comprehensive global international migration system nor does there exist a specific and universal convention governing migrants' rights and governments' responsibilities. Rather, migrants are given haphazard protection under general human rights law and advocacy, labour rights agreements, and a patchwork of other regional standards. It was only in 2016 that this gap began to be addressed when the UN General Assembly passed the New York Declaration for Refugees and Migrants, leading to the incorporation of the IOM into the UN System and the adoption of the non-binding Global Compact for Safe, Orderly and Regular Migration by 164 countries in 2018.

During the 21st century, globalization has created new opportunities and incentives for international migration. It has brought with it the development of improved transportation and telecommunications, including the expanding use of social media and network sites, and new diaspora networks comprising overseas immigrant communities with close links to their home communities. But this century has also seen the dramatic growth in human trafficking and trans-continental people smuggling. Refugees and migrants in the Middle East, Africa, Asia, and Central America and the Caribbean now traverse vast deserts and dangerous seas and land routes in the hope of achieving a safer and better life in Europe, North America, Australia, and elsewhere. These trends have contributed dramatically to growing South to North migration and refugee flows since the 1980s.

In recent years, it has become increasingly difficult to distinguish between refugees and migrants in some situations. While economic hardship may be the proximate cause of flight, many migrants are vulnerable and in need of humanitarian protection, particularly from people smugglers and other dangers, irrespective of their legal status. Others would be at risk of persecution if returned home, and may thus qualify for refugee status.

As legal migration opportunities in the Global North diminish, people who might previously have migrated legally are turning to traffickers to travel to and enter countries in the Global North. They then frequently have to claim asylum in an effort to stay. As we will discuss in Chapter 4, many governments in the Global North now impose stricter limits on migrants, employ additional tactics to curb asylum claims, and apply heightened scrutiny to such claims.

Western governments have also adopted a series of migration control measures to deter new arrivals of both migrants and asylum seekers. These include tightening pre-arrival screening at airports and seaports, routinely detaining asylum seekers and migrants, restricting their access to health and other social services, deporting migrants and asylum seekers to so-called 'safe third countries', and even deploying warships to intercept boatloads of refugees and migrants on the high seas.

In addition, in an effort to curb the numbers of asylum seekers and migrants trying to reach European and US territory, Western governments have also negotiated often dubious deals with transit countries in the Global South in order to curb new arrivals in the Global North. For example, in 2016 EU states agreed to relocate asylum seekers stranded in Greece to a politically unstable situation in Turkey in exchange for a huge payment of funds to Ankara and a promise to reopen negotiations over loosening travel restrictions to the EU for Turkish citizens. Similarly, in 2017, Italy and Libya reached a highly criticized agreement enabling Italy to return African migrants and asylum seekers to Libya. Many of these returnees have ended up in inhumane detention centres where they are ill-treated and physically abused. There have even been reports of some returned migrants being sold into slavery. At the same time, East and Central European governments, led mostly by populist politicians, have erected walls, barbed wire fences, and other barriers to try to keep asylum seekers and migrants from crossing into their countries. Similar walls and strict border controls were being constructed along the US–Mexico border and implemented by the United States under President Trump.

António Guterres, the former UN High Commissioner for Refugees and currently the Secretary-General of the United Nations, has argued that, together, these dangerous conditions and trends raise questions about the applicability of conventional refugee definitions and concepts to current realities experienced by many migrants today. He argues that by strictly distinguishing between the two categories of people on the move (migrants and refugees) we risk ignoring the need for a more nuanced understanding of the often unjust social, political, and economic structures prompting people to migrate or to flee their home countries. Nor does refugee law take account of the similar dangers and extreme risks both groups often face during their journeys to safety and a new life. Refugee and human rights organizations argue that policymakers may have to consider amending the refugee definition to take account of these developments and to broaden the international protection for vulnerable and at-risk migrants as well as for refugees.

Yet a wider group of people are driven from their homes due to the collapse of governments and economies. During recent years, numerous internal or intrastate conflicts, in which particular rebel groups and non-state actors such as warlords, militias, rebel groups, terrorists, criminal networks, and gangs have fought for control over the state and its resources, have emerged across the world. The governance capacity of many of these states has effectively collapsed. There are no jobs, the country's currency is worthless, and corruption, violence, and fear reign unchecked. Such states are often designated as fragile or failed and are chronically weak, incompetent, and lack the capacity to govern or protect their citizens effectively. These situations displace huge numbers of so-called **'survival migrants'** who are often left unprotected and unassisted as they do not qualify as refugees.

Afghanistan is but one example of a long-standing weak state which is unable or fails to impose the rule of law and to protect its civilians from conflict, persecution, and impoverishment. For the past four decades, Afghanistan has been a poor, drought-inflicted, and conflict-ridden country where rival warlords have competed for power and have ruthlessly killed their opponents as well as civilians. In recent years, fighting between Islamic State (IS) and Taliban forces and between these militants and the US and European militaries has displaced tens of thousands of civilians. Even in the country's capital, Kabul, Taliban and IS have struck with suicide bombs and killed and injured civilians with impunity. Almost permanent conflict and persecution over the past several decades have driven millions of Afghans into exile in neighbouring Pakistan and Iran and farther afield to Europe and other Western countries. As a consequence of continuing conflict in the country, a growing number of Afghans have become internally displaced and are given inadequate protection and assistance by their government.

In recent years people have increasingly fled other weak, failing, and collapsing states such as Venezuela, Zimbabwe, Somalia, Yemen, Chad, South Sudan, the Democratic Republic of the Congo, Iraq, and Haiti, among others. Large numbers of people in Central America, including women and children, have been compelled to flee life-threatening situations such as starvation, incapacitating poverty, and unchecked violence and physical attacks by criminal gangs because their own governments are unwilling or unable to provide even minimal protection of their basic rights.

State fragility opens up a range of questions about the scope of who should be entitled to temporary or permanent asylum and protection beyond the scope of the 1951 Convention. Alexander Betts, a professor at the Refugee Studies Centre at the University of Oxford, has termed those who flee failing states as 'survival migrants'. He has pointed out that there is a need for UNHCR and states to reflect on how they engage with populations who leave countries that are unwilling and unable to provide the most fundamental human rights and protection for their citizens. Whether people fleeing state fragility or state failure should be assisted and protected by UNHCR and other agencies continues to be one of the most pressing questions facing the international community today.

A relatively recent and increasingly important and serious category of forced migration is that of **environmental displacement** caused by climate change, natural disasters, and rising seas. There has been a dramatic increase in the number people forced to migrate as a result of environmental impacts. The increase in the number of floods, droughts, hurricanes, violent storms, as well as other natural disasters in particularly vulnerable countries exacerbates access to livelihoods and increases competition for scarce essential resources such as water and open grazing lands. These events and tensions not only cause human rights violations and conflicts among local populations in the Global South but are also fast becoming a major source of displacement today. In the early 21st century, natural disasters have uprooted and displaced millions of people throughout Asia, Africa, the Pacific, and the Middle East, as well as in the Caribbean, Central America, and Mexico. Even the United States and other parts of the developed world have experienced major damage and loss of life as a consequence of more frequent and violent storms.

Unless effective collective action is taken to address the issue of climate and environmental change now there will be even greater numbers of natural disasters, conflicts, and further internal and external displacements in the very near future. For example, it is estimated that at least half of the land mass in Bangladesh, a country with 163 million people and the most densely populated country in the world, will be submerged by rising seas and violent storms in the near future. Poverty, scarcity of land and water, rapid population growth, degradation of human habitat, and environmental pressures are already driving large numbers of people from Bangladesh to India and other nearby countries.

Elsewhere in Asia, Jakarta, the capital city of Indonesia with a population of over 30 million people, and with limited resources and poor infrastructure, is at risk of massive flooding and sinking under the rising Java Sea. A similar fate awaits many countries in Africa, South Asia, many of the island nations in the Pacific, the Caribbean, and elsewhere, creating large-scale environmental refugee crises. Such cataclysmic events also have the potential to cause conflicts leading to more forced displacement, food insecurity, and interstate tensions. Some estimates suggest that the number of people displaced across borders due to the consequences of climate change could reach 200 million by the year 2050.

While most people displaced across borders by natural disasters fall outside the scope of the 1951 Refugee Convention and do not have the same rights as refugees, UNHCR and other agencies are increasingly addressing humanitarian crises and displacement created by recent major natural disasters by providing disaster assistance and raising public awareness of this enormous and rapidly growing problem.

Among the world's science community there is a growing recognition that the environment, climate change, and human displacement are closely related and that there is a need to more strongly and effectively address this issue at the global and regional levels. For example, in 2012 the Nansen Initiative and its 'Agenda for the protection of cross-border displaced persons in the context of disaster and climate change' was endorsed by over a hundred governments. Similar initiatives to strengthen the protection available to people affected by environmental and disaster displacement are required both for people who remain at home and for those who are forced to leave their country during such crises.

A 2020 decision by the UN Human Rights Committee may significantly enhance the rights of people who flee the consequences of climate change. In considering the case of an individual who fled to New Zealand due to the effects of climate change, the UN found that, while the individual is not a refugee, he should not be returned to his country of origin if he were to face threats to his human rights upon return. In this way, persons displaced by climate change may soon enjoy the same safeguard against forcible return as enjoyed by refugees. As emphasized in Chapter 7, addressing the needs of persons displaced by climate change and future environmental disasters is the most important challenge confronting the international community both at present and in future years.

Chapter 2
Refugees: a short history

While refugees are one of the hallmarks of contemporary society, hope for the future protection of refugees relies, at least partially, on our understanding of history. Mobility has been a defining feature of human history since our ancestors first travelled from the Olduvai Gorge more than 300,000 years ago. War, exile, and refugees have been documented features of history since the Greek and Roman classical eras and are featured in the epic poetry of the era.

In fact, the history of every region of the world tells of the movement of people due to conflict and persecution. Throughout all periods of human history, people have been forcibly displaced and have fled their homes as a consequence of political, ethnic, and religious persecution, and wars.

Furthermore, the practice of offering some form of protection, political belonging and rights for the displaced by receiving societies and religious institutions has an equally long history. Every major world religion contains teachings on the importance of providing protection to those in need. Historian Michael Marrus has noted that before the 20th century, some refugees were regarded as assets rather than liabilities. Political, religious, and military leaders granted refuge to people of religious, geopolitical, or ideological views similar to their own, and rulers viewed control over large populations, along with natural resources and territory itself, as an index of power and national greatness.

In later periods of European history, however, states used mass expulsion as a means for dealing with unwanted national and religious minorities. One of the best-known examples occurred in 1492 in Spain when the Catholic monarchs issued the Alhambra Edict which led to the expulsion of over 150,000 Muslims (so-called Moors) and Sephardic Jews.

Refugees became a significant international issue in Europe during the formation of the modern state system in the 17th century. During the Thirty Years War (1618–48), which was fought over religious liberty in Protestant and Catholic kingdoms in Europe, as many as 11 million people were reportedly murdered, many of them burned at the stake. It was only in 1648, when the Peace of Westphalia ended Europe's brutal religious wars, that it was agreed that subjects in Europe whose religion differed from that of their monarchs were permitted to leave their country in safety and with their property and possessions.

Just four decades later, in 1685, Louis XIV of Catholic France revoked the Edict of Nantes that had allowed Protestant Huguenots to practise their religion openly. Those who remained in France faced persecution. During the next twenty years, some 200,000 Huguenots fled France with their belongings to seek safety in neighbouring European Protestant countries, particularly England. Significantly, the term *refugees* was used for the first time to describe those who fled.

In later years, several prominent refugee crises occurred. For example, during the French Revolution in 1789 refugees fled to neighbouring countries to avoid political persecution at home. And nearly a hundred years later some 2 million Jews were forced into exile by violent attacks and pogroms in Russia and the Baltic region.

During a period of European colonization in the 18th and 19th centuries in Africa, the Middle East, and Asia, Western powers and their local officials frequently oversaw mass displacements and even genocides of native populations. For example, in the Belgium colony of the Congo, King Leopold oversaw the mass murder of an estimated 10 million Africans. Colonial powers also undertook the emergence of a worldwide slavery trade involving the forced transportation of millions of Africans and other populations to Europe, the United States, Latin America, and the Caribbean. In later years, Western colonial powers initiated the forced movement of millions of indentured labourers and servants from India, China, Japan, and other countries to work on colonial plantations around the world.

While far from exhaustive, even this small glimpse into history shows that refugees have been a feature of human history and the emergence of the modern state system. However, before the 20th century there were no formal, institutional standards for the protection of refugees as we know it today. For the most part, refugees were left to fend for themselves and were reliant on the benevolence of the rulers of the territory in which they sought protection. European citizens enjoyed the protection of their sovereigns or national governments, but once they fled their home countries and became refugees they were totally bereft of protection except when other states or private institutions or individuals might elect to provide it. Asylum was a gift of the crown, the church, and municipalities; and forcibly displaced individuals and groups could expect no response to claims of asylum or protection premised on human or political rights.

Evolution of the modern international refugee system

During the late 19th and early 20th centuries, both the causes and dimensions of the refugee problem began to change radically. The evolving destructiveness and brutality of international warfare, and the frequent occurrence of famines and forced starvation as a weapon of curbing dissent and waging war, became the immediate causes of most refugee movements.

Although war had always generated large numbers of refugees, only in the 20th century did international conflict affect entire civilian populations. With the advent of wider technological, economic, and social changes, the scale and destructiveness of military conflict grew enormously. Enemy civilians as well as opposing armed forces became military targets. The elimination of the distinction between combatants and non-combatants produced vast numbers of new refugees. The First World War (1914–18) killed some 11 million combatants and displaced millions more.

Another prominent cause of refugee movements during the early part of the 20th century was the collapse of multinational empires and the formation, consolidation, and expansion of the state system. The Habsburg, Romanov, Ottoman, and Hohenzollern empires succumbed to the pressures and conflicts that accompanied the transition from imperial social and political orders to successor nation-states.

With the dismantling of these multi-ethnic empires into separate nation-states, masses of people were excluded from citizenship in the new national states on grounds of language, location, ethnicity, or religious affiliation. Many of the newly formed governments in Central Europe, the Balkans, and the Baltics tried to eliminate the old order and consolidate their power by creating culturally and politically homogeneous populations. Elsewhere, in a continuation of a policy of 'ethnic cleansing' begun in the late 19th century, the Turks engaged in massacres and genocides of the Armenians and Kurds. During 1914 to 1919, between 500,000 and 1 million Armenians were killed and survivors fled to Soviet Armenia, Syria, and other parts of Europe and the Middle East.

Western powers attempted, in a series of Minority Treaties, to provide for the elementary rights of ethnic minorities who were threatened as a result of the redrawing of national boundaries. However, as the global economy deteriorated, minority populations quickly became scapegoats and vulnerable to mass deportation. Governments defined broad categories of people as belonging to the nation-state and relegated others to the ranks of outsiders and aliens who threatened national and cultural cohesion.

As nations redefined their borders and identities and the 'unmixing of peoples' was imposed on sometimes reluctant populations, millions of people were rendered stateless. Conflict between Greece and Turkey led to the massacre of both Christians and Muslims during the Graeco-Turkish war of 1920–2. In 1923 Greece and Turkey enacted the first compulsory population exchange in modern history. Some 2 million people, Christians in Turkey and Muslims in Greece, were forcibly uprooted from their homes without being offered any other choice.

To the chaos in south-eastern Europe and Asia Minor were added huge refugee movements generated by the collapse of Tsarist Russia, the Russian Civil War, the Russo-Polish War, and the Soviet famine of 1921. These cataclysmic events resulted in the death of masses of Russians and dispersed between 1 and 2 million people from the Russian empire mostly to Germany and France but also to the far reaches of the world including China and North America.

The Russian refugees included not only those perceived to be enemies of the Communist Party but also soldiers of the defeated White Russian armies who had participated in the Russian Civil War, civilians fleeing the chaos and famine brought about by the Revolution and Civil War, ethnic Russians fleeing newly independent Poland and the Baltic States, and Russian Jews facing persecution. The cumulative result of these events was one of the largest displacements of peoples in Europe in modern times. By the early 1920s, the Soviet Union issued decrees that revoked the citizenship of many of its inhabitants. Escaping war and famine at home, vast numbers of Russians wandered all over Europe, where they became a source of interstate friction because of their lack of national identity papers.

The sheer numbers of these refugees, their expulsion from their homeland, and the long years of their displaced wanderings made their collective fate in the 20th century qualitatively different from that of other groups forced into exile by earlier political or religious upheavals. Refugee movements far exceeded the limited capacity of individual governments to respond adequately. It was within this context that the first rudimentary international organizations were formed to promote the protection and resettlement of refugees.

This early response was initially devised as a way to address the mass displacement caused by the First World War, the Russian Revolution, and the collapse of the Habsburg and Ottoman Empires. In 1921, the League of Nations appointed Fridtjof Nansen, the world-famous Norwegian explorer, to be the first High Commissioner for Refugees. Governments originally mandated that Nansen's Office be limited to direct relief efforts to respond to the growing famine in Russia, that League funds be spent only on administration and not on direct relief, and that refugee assistance be considered temporary. Not only did governments keep the mandate of Nansen and successor High Commissioners deliberately narrow, they also refrained from adopting any universal definition of the term 'refugee' for fear of opening the door to international recognition of political dissidents in any state.

Despite these impediments, Nansen undertook a number of initiatives on behalf of refugees. In 1921 he directed relief efforts to respond to a growing famine in Russia and in 1922 he oversaw an exchange of Greeks after the Graeco-Turkish war. Nansen also established the 'Nansen passports' for stateless refugees, primarily Russians: a substitute travel document issued for refugees who were unable to obtain documentation from their own governments.

Under Nansen the international refugee system eventually grew to encompass refugee settlement, employment opportunities, emigration, and linkage of refugee assistance with economic development. The International Labour Organization (ILO) developed a comprehensive set of provisions covering employment and social services. These initiatives led to the drafting of a convention in 1933 which later listed a number of rights such as access to education and employment in the receiving country and travel documents. Although the language of this and other conventions at the time was purposely limited to benefit narrowly defined national groups of displaced persons and provided only minimal protection for the members of these groups, this was a step towards the formulation of more permanent international laws and institutions directed at refugees.

Nansen died in 1930. During the next ten years, the international refugee system proved incapable of dealing with a growing refugee problem. With the rise of fascism and populist leaders in Germany, Italy, Spain, and Portugal during the 1930s and the adoption of state policies to forcibly expel those considered inferior, Europe was flooded with new groups of refugees.

In Germany, the main targets were not only political opponents, such as communists, Social Democrats, antifascist intellectuals, and pacifists, but also mentally and physically disabled people and members of so-called 'racially inferior' population groups—mainly Jews, Slavs, and gypsies. Major waves of emigration took place after the initial Nazi takeover in 1933, again after the passage of the Nuremberg Laws in 1935, and a third time after the devastation of Kristallnacht in 1938. The Nazis began deporting

Jews to Poland after the annexation of that country and in October 1941 the 'Final Solution'—to exterminate the Jewish people—was adopted as state policy.

The rise of fascism in other European countries also created refugee movements, particularly from Spain. Some 400,000 Spanish Republicans fleeing Civil War and the Franco regime took refuge in France. Much smaller numbers of refugees fled fascist regimes in Mussolini's Italy and Salazar's Portugal.

Refugee movements in Europe during this period would have been far greater had it not been for the exit controls and emigration restrictions imposed by a number of governments. Only a trickle of people were able to flee the Soviet Union, for example, compared with the estimated 20 to 40 million people who died there during Stalin's murderous 'Red Terror'. Outside Europe, over 100 million people were forcibly displaced in Asia and the Pacific during the 1930s and 1940s as a consequence of the brutal Japanese military invasion of China and Southeast Asia and widespread conflict in the Pacific region.

The failure of international cooperation regarding refugees during the 1930s is traceable not only to the weakness of the League of Nations and the refugee agencies under its auspices after Nansen's death, but also to the absence of any consistent or coherent international commitment to resolving refugee problems. Instead, there was a broad consensus in almost every industrialized nation, particularly during the Great Depression, that national interests were best served by imposing rigid limits on immigration, that humanitarian initiatives on behalf of refugees had to be limited by tight fiscal constraints, and that employment opportunities for the nation's own citizens should be prioritized in economically difficult times. Moreover, it was widely believed that no particular foreign policy benefits would accrue from putting political and moral pressure on refugee-generating countries or from accepting their unwanted dissidents and minority groups. These views were also fully operative in the United States and in Commonwealth countries such as Canada and Australia, which prior to the First World War had accepted a substantial number of Europe's forced migrants.

Restrictionism was exacerbated by deepening worldwide economic depression and massive unemployment. In the United States, the Immigration Acts of 1921 and 1924 established a quota system designed to limit total immigration and to ensure a certain ethnic composition among each year's newcomers. The British Dominions enacted restrictions aimed at keeping their population British. Australia restricted immigration by non-British migrants, excluded Asians altogether, and promoted schemes to bring in British settlers. In Canada and Latin America, restrictive policies became general policy.

With Adolf Hitler's accession to power in Germany in 1933, Jewish refugees began to flee the country in increasing numbers. As a consequence, the League established yet another refugee organization, the High Commissioner for Refugees from Germany. Because Germany was a member state of the League of Nations and other League members were concerned about Germany's sensibilities, the new refugee organization was set up outside of the League's formal structure. The new High Commissioner, James McDonald, was instructed to avoid discussing the causes or stressing the political dimensions of the refugee problem with Berlin. Moreover, the Commissioner's tasks were restricted to negotiating with host governments concerning settlement and emigration plans and the questions of work permits and travel documents. Finally, in contrast to its predecessor, the new refugee organization did not even receive funding from the League for its administrative expenses. Not surprisingly, McDonald could accomplish little in these circumstances and he resigned in 1936. In his letter of resignation, McDonald referred to the need to set aside state sovereignty in favour of humanitarian imperatives. 'When domestic politics threaten the demoralization and exile of hundreds of thousands of human beings, considerations of diplomatic correctness must yield to those of common humanity.' They did not.

The two offices for refugees—the International Nansen Office and the High Commissioner for Refugees from Germany—were consolidated into what became the High Commissioner for Refugees. The power and influence of this successor institution was even more limited than those that preceded it. In 1938, under pressure from Jewish groups and private voluntary agencies, US President Franklin D. Roosevelt called for an international conference at Évian in France to consider ways of resettling Jews who had fled from Germany and Austria. At Évian, the United States made no new pledges for an increased quota for Jewish refugees. Delegates from other countries noted that the movement of Jewish refugees was 'disturbing to the general economy' since 'those in flight were seeking refuge at a time of serious unemployment'. The Évian Conference yielded no new resettlement places for Jewish refugees. The only substantive result of the conference was the establishment of the Intergovernmental Committee on Refugees to facilitate any resettlement of refugees from Germany or Austria, of which there were few.

Unlike many earlier refugee movements, those uprooted in the interwar period defied quick solutions. During the 1930s, the world's leaders were essentially impotent in confronting Europe's dictators, and the response to the refugee problem by both governments and international organizations was politicized and selective. Throughout this period, assistance and protection were temporary and limited to certain groups.

Nevertheless, the institutions created to respond to refugee problems during the interwar period did leave one lasting and important legacy. Twenty years of organizational growth and interstate collaboration had firmly established the idea that refugees constituted victims of human rights abuses for whom the world had a special responsibility. Moreover, the first international cooperative efforts on behalf of refugees and the establishment and evolution of the international refugee agencies of the period provided the foundations on which successor institutions would be built.

The Second World War and the early post-war refugee crisis

The most dramatic period of mass displacement in the history of Europe and Asia occurred in the 1940s as a result of war and political upheaval. A US State Department report prepared in early 1945 described the situation in Europe at the end of the war as '[one] of the greatest population movements of history taking place before our eyes. As the German retreat has rolled westward before the oncoming Soviet troops and as the allies have pushed eastward on the western front, millions of people have been uprooted and are fleeing toward the center of Germany.' This flow not only included the 20 to 30 million people uprooted during the war, but also the removal of at least 13 to 14 million Germans returning from countries outside the Reich, and more than 4 million war fugitives who fled before the oncoming Soviet and Allied troops. In total an estimated 60 million refugees flooded continental Europe.

The influx of so many refugees and other displaced people in such a short time into an area where most of the physical infrastructure had been bombed and destroyed put huge pressures on West European states, particularly West Germany, and on the Allied military authorities responsible for administering significant areas of former enemy territory.

Decisions taken in the months that followed on how to respond to the challenges associated with mass displacement laid the foundation for the international refugee system that endures to this day. It is for this reason that it is helpful to understand this sequence of events in some detail.

Late in the Second World War, the Western powers established the United Nations Relief and Rehabilitation Agency (UNRRA) to provide temporary emergency assistance for the millions of displaced persons (DPs). Working directly under Allied military command, UNRRA assisted civilian nationals uprooted and made homeless by the war. UNRRA had no power to resettle refugees and displaced persons to third countries. The goal was simply to return home as soon as possible all the people who had been displaced by the conflict in Europe. At the Yalta conference in February 1945, the US, Britain, and the Soviet Union paved the way for large-scale repatriations to the Soviet Union, and at the Potsdam Conference in August 1945 they provided for the return to Germany of its ethnic minorities in Poland, Czechoslovakia, and Hungary. Consequently UNRRA aided Allied military forces in identifying displaced persons, separating them into broad national categories, putting them into trucks and railway boxcars, and shipping them back to the countries from which they had originally come without regard to their individual wishes. During the first five months after the war, UNRRA and the Allied military command managed to repatriate nearly three-quarters of the displaced people in Europe. Many returnees ended up in Stalin's labour camps and others faced political persecution.

Not surprisingly, the issue of repatriation of displaced persons erupted into a major East–West controversy and relations between the Western powers and the Soviet Union rapidly deteriorated. Repatriation touched on the fundamental ideological conflicts dividing the Soviet Union and the United States and its allies. The communist bloc rejected outright the idea that citizens of Eastern European countries could have any valid reason for opposing return and maintained that those who resisted were war criminals, quislings, and traitors.

The United States, which provided 70 per cent of UNRRA funds, became strongly critical of the organization's operations, in particular its repatriation policies as well as its economic rehabilitation programmes in communist bloc countries in Eastern Europe. In 1947, the US terminated its assistance funds to UNRRA and worked to create a new American-led International Refugee Organization (IRO), which had as its chief function not repatriation but the overseas resettlement of refugees and displaced persons. In the subsequent debate within the UN General Assembly, the Western states insisted that the mandate of IRO be broad enough to offer protection to individuals with valid objections to repatriation, including those based on 'persecution, or fear, based on reasonable grounds, of persecution because of race, religion, nationality or political opinions', and 'objections of a political nature, judged by the organization to be valid'. Previously, international organizations had dealt only with specific groups of refugees, such as Russian or German refugees, and governments had never attempted to formulate a general definition of the term 'refugee'. For the first time, therefore, the international community made refugee eligibility dependent on the individual rather than group membership and accepted the individual's right to flee from political persecution to a safe country.

With the opening-up of a major resettlement programme led by IRO, the number of repatriations to Eastern Europe was reduced to a small trickle. Because the war-torn countries of Western Europe were incapable of accepting all the remaining displaced persons, pressure was put on the United States, Canada, Australia, and even countries in Latin America, the Middle East, and Africa to make available resettlement places for Europe's DPs. During the four and a half years of IRO operations, the United States received 31.7 per cent of the refugees resettled; Australia 17.5; Israel 12.7; Canada 11.9; Britain 8.3; Western Europe 6.8; and the countries of Latin America 6.5.

By the end of IRO's tenure, the selective refugee admissions policies of receiving states left behind some 400,000 people, most of whom were still in Displaced Persons camps scattered throughout Western Europe. The scandal of these camps was to be the subject of criticism in the West and elsewhere for the next decade and a half. Beyond this 'hard-core' group, the number of refugees continued to grow during the 1950s, with large numbers of persons fleeing East European communist countries for resettlement in the West. By the end of the decade some 900,000 European refugees had been absorbed by West European governments, 461,000 had been resettled in the United States, and a further 523,000 by other countries.

In addition to events in Europe, from the late 1930s to the end of the Second World War in 1945 huge numbers of people were displaced in other parts of the world. East and South Asia, in particular, were the sites of major atrocities and refugee crises. Over a period of six weeks in late 1937, the Japanese military brutally murdered many hundreds of thousands of Chinese soldiers and civilians and raped thousands of Chinese women in what became known as the Nanjing Massacre. During the course of the Second World War, an estimated 6 million Chinese, Indonesians, Koreans, Filipinos, Burmese, and Indochinese among others, including Western prisoners of war, were killed by the Japanese military. Following these massacres and the huge displacements of people in China, Southeast Asia, and the Pacific during the Second World War, civil war in China between forces of the Chinese communists and those of the Chinese Nationalists displaced hundreds of thousands more Chinese, many of whom fled to the British Crown Colony of Hong Kong or to the newly formed Republic of China on Taiwan.

In South Asia, the partition of India and the creation of the new state of Pakistan in 1947–8 were accompanied by widespread communal violence between Muslims, Hindus, and Sikhs and forced over 12 million people from their homes. In 1948, the conflict between Jewish settlers and the local Palestinian population gave rise to the flight of over 700,000 Palestinians to neighbouring countries and territories. Similarly, the Korean War (1950–3) uprooted millions of Koreans, most of whom fled to South Korea, which was under the control of UN forces. To respond to these crises, two new international relief organizations were formed: the UN Relief and Works Agency for Palestinian Refugees (UNRWA) in 1949 and the UN Korean Relief Organization in 1951, both of which received large-scale funding from the US.

The contemporary global refugee regime

By the late 1940s, the newly created United Nations recognized the need to extend the existing international treaties and organizations regarding refugees particularly to meet the growing post-war refugee problem in Europe. The result was a process that established the contemporary 'global refugee regime': the core principles and institutions created by states to try to make responses to refugees more reliable and to ensure protection and solutions for refugees.

The principles of the regime were contained in the 1951 Convention relating to the Status of Refugees. Reflecting the geopolitical interests of the United States and its European allies at that time, the drafters of the Convention limited its coverage to those Europeans who had fled their home countries before 1951. The refugee regime was shaped to find protection and solutions for those persecuted as well as those displaced by the Second World War and by the subsequent emergence of the Cold War. Despite the numerous dramatic refugee crises outside Europe at the time, the government representatives who drafted the Convention limited the focus of the document specifically to refugees in Europe who had fled from events which occurred before 1951. The framers of the Convention also excluded any protection for internally displaced persons. It was not until 1967 that governments approved a Protocol to the Convention that extended its benefits to later refugee events in other parts of the world beyond Europe.

Six months prior to the establishment of the Refugee Convention, in December 1950, UNHCR was created and was given a mandate to ensure protection for refugees and to work with governments to find a solution to their plight. Initially, UNHCR had a meagre budget and was restricted to working only with European refugees who had fled their home countries before 1951. Despite these early restrictions imposed on UNHCR by governments, UNHCR became the lead agency in the international response to the world's first major Cold War refugee emergency in Hungary in 1956. Tens of thousands of Hungarians fled across the border with Austria to escape the imposition of communist rule by invading Soviet soldiers and tanks. In response, UNHCR was active in steering a major resettlement effort in North America and Europe for over 100,000 Hungarian refugees.

UNHCR also became partially engaged in post-1951 refugee crises outside Europe involving refugees fleeing the communist regime in the Peoples' Republic of China to Hong Kong in the mid-1950s and Algerian refugees who had fled to Tunisia during the Algerian War in the late 1950s. But apart from these exceptions, UNHCR mostly avoided involvement in displacement and forced expulsion in parts of the world outside Europe, including the expulsion of large numbers of overseas Chinese refugees from Indonesia to China, the exodus of Tibetan refugees from China to India following the departure of the Dalai Lama in the late 1950s, and expulsions in other parts of Asia and in Africa.

UNHCR was not static, however, and from the 1960s on it assumed new roles to deal with displacement caused by de-colonization in Africa, the spread of the Cold War beyond Europe to other regions, and including internal conflicts and surrogate conflicts between the two superpowers in Asia and Africa. As noted in Chapter 1, during these subsequent decades the term 'refugee' was widened in practice beyond the 1951 legal definition to cover some of the people in diverse situations who need assistance and protection.

Growth of the global refugee regime

For decades, the principles of the refugee regime provided a framework, which—with some significant exceptions—ensured safe haven for millions of refugees in Europe, Africa, Latin America, and most of Asia. During this same period, UNHCR, as the key institution of the regime, underwent an extraordinary growth in the scale and scope of its work. From the 1960s, UNHCR became increasingly involved in refugee situations as a consequence of wars of liberation in the Global South. Violent decolonization and post-independence strife generated vast numbers of refugees in Africa and Asia and UNHCR assumed an ever-greater role in providing refugees with material assistance as well as international protection. During the 1970s, mass exoduses from East Pakistan, Uganda, Cyprus, and Indochina, highly politicized human rights crises in Chile, Brazil, and Argentina, and the repatriation of refugees and internally displaced persons in southern Sudan, all contributed to an expansion of UNHCR's mission around the world.

During the late 1970s and 1980s, UNHCR shifted away from its traditional focus on legal protection and limited material assistance and assumed a growing role in providing assistance to millions of refugees in protracted refugee situations in Southeast Asia, Mexico and Central America, South Asia, the Horn of Africa, and southern Africa. With huge increases in funding from the US and other Western states, UNHCR was tasked with assisting and protecting refugees who were displaced by political regimes supported and financed by the former Soviet Union or its allies. Solutions to these protracted refugee crises were elusive and large sums of funding were spent on financing the care and maintenance of refugee camps in countries neighbouring states at war.

By the mid-1980s, regional host countries and Western governments also began to feel the impact of larger numbers of asylum seekers travelling from the Global South to Europe and North America. In previous decades, most refugees appearing in the West had fled well-publicized persecution in communist countries and were accepted by governments with little scrutiny into their motives for departure. The intensification of the Cold War across the Global South in the 1980s, coupled with the expansion of jet air and other means of travel, allowed tens of thousands of refugees to travel from regions of conflict in developing countries to claim asylum in Europe and North America. Particularly disturbing to Western governments was the fact that asylum applicants increasingly bypassed established refugee-processing channels. Unlike the millions who had endured the rigours of camp life in the developing world, the new asylum seekers either independently took the initiative to seek safety in the West through legal channels or turned to migrant-smuggling organizations for false documents and to provide them with transport to travel to industrialized countries. Western governments considered such activities illegal and branded many asylum seekers as 'opportunists, bogus refugees and queue jumpers'.

In the aftermath of the Cold War during the early 1990s, the former Soviet Union and many of its allies around the world collapsed and a range of brutal internal conflicts, genocides, and campaigns of ethnic cleansing in the Balkans, Central Africa, Myanmar, Afghanistan, and the Caucuses generated millions more new refugees and internally displaced people. In response to these crises, UNHCR assumed a wider role in providing massive humanitarian relief in intrastate conflicts and engaged in several major repatriation operations in Africa, Asia, Central America, and the Balkans. At the same time, the international community was increasingly confronted with the growing problem of internal displacement of people uprooted by conflict and persecution but who did not cross an international border. Initially, UNHCR was reluctant to expand its mandate to include the protection of internally displaced persons but the Office eventually recognized that many of those displaced within the borders of their own countries were at severe risk and otherwise indistinguishable from refugees.

In the early 21st century, in the context of the 'War on Terror' and Western occupations in Afghanistan and Iraq, UNHCR became engulfed in responding to yet more refugee emergencies. UNHCR also took on ever greater responsibility for the victims of several major natural disasters such as tsunamis in Southeast Asia. From 2005, the Office assumed formal responsibility for the protection of conflict-induced internally displaced persons. By 2019, the Office had developed an enormous global agenda and had over 16,803 staff in 134 countries around the world and an annual budget of US$8.6 billion. This represents extraordinary growth from UNHCR's origins in 1950 of a global staff of 30 and an annual budget of US$300,000.

In recent years, forced migration has continued to be a major feature of world politics. While the international community has seen large refugee crises before, the crucial issue today is how badly governments, the UN Security Council, UNHCR, and other international actors are coping with the global refugee situation and what they should do about it. Today's brutal internal conflicts and refugee crises in Syria, Iraq, Yemen, South Sudan, the Democratic Republic of the Congo, Afghanistan, Myanmar, and throughout most countries of West and Central Africa and Central America impact millions of civilians caught up in these events. During the past several decades, huge numbers of people around the world have been forcibly displaced as a result of political or religious persecution, widespread discrimination on the basis of gender identity or sexual orientation, ethnicity, and endless conflicts and criminal violence involving both state and non-state actors. Authoritarian regimes, human rights violations, the activities of radical militant non-state actors such as Al-Qaeda, the Taliban, Islamic State (IS), Hezbollah, Boko Haram, Al-Shabab, and other radical groups have led to greater numbers of refugees. At the same time, the rapid increase in the number and frequency of environmental crises and natural disasters and the rise of so-called 'failed states' will lead to further mass displacements of vulnerable people across the world in the near future.

How can the international community respond to the growing challenge of ensuring protection and solutions for refugees and other forced migrants? It is important to start by understanding the diverse causes of contemporary forced displacement.

Chapter 3
Causes of refugee movements

While each of the 26 million refugees in the world today has their own story as to why they needed to flee their countries, there are a range of forces that drive contemporary refugee movements. The traditional cause of refugee movements—persecution—is now just one factor amongst an array of forces that cause people to flee their homelands. The majority of mass movements today are caused by internal conflicts, and ethnic cleansing, genocide and politicide, religious, cultural, and ethnic intolerance and conflict, sharp socio-economic inequalities, and increasingly by conflict-induced famine, mass starvation, and climate change.

As noted throughout this book, climate change and the increasing occurrence of environmental disasters are likely to be a major cause of forced displacement in the coming decades. In parts of Asia and Africa, global warming, rising seas, violent storms, and climate change have brought floods and droughts and displaced masses of people and have raised tensions and caused conflicts between pastoralists and farmers and others over dwindling national resources such as water, food, and grazing land. Left unaddressed, these tensions will foster further conflicts and displacements now and in the future.

Likewise, the difficulty of building resilient and responsive state structures in the context of deep ethnic divisions and economic inequality has resulted in much of the domestic conflict and political instability that many developing countries currently experience. Moreover, international terrorist organizations have thrived in these contexts of instability and multiplied in recent years. They have deliberately and brutally displaced entire minority and religious communities in villages and cities across the Middle East, Africa, and Asia. Finally, gang violence and intimidation, particularly in Central and South America and in other regions of the world, have driven increasing numbers of people into exile.

The proliferation of internal conflicts characterized by strong ethnic, religious, and communal hostilities, the actions of warlords, and the widespread availability of small arms and other instruments of violence constitute a massive stimulus to militarization and conflict in the Global South and other parts of the world. Combatants also routinely use instruments of terror and torture, racism, misogyny, slavery, and malicious behaviour such as mass murder and acts of terror to achieve conquest over their rivals and to eliminate entire religious or ethnic groups.

As a consequence of such violence, there has been a proliferation of so-called complex emergencies that combine internal conflicts with large-scale displacement of people. Today's refugee crises are marked by life-threatening food and medical shortages and enforced starvation on a scale not seen in generations. Combatants routinely use starvation and food insecurity as weapons of war. Children and other vulnerable people are hit hardest by such shortages particularly when they are widely used as weapons. Conflict-induced famines in Yemen, Syria, South Sudan, the Democratic Republic of the Congo, and the Central African Republic, among other states, have killed hundreds of thousands of vulnerable children and elderly people and others in villages, cities, and countries under attack.

Responses to these diverse drivers of displacement go well beyond the tools of the global refugee regime. They speak to core questions of governance, peace and security, peacebuilding, development, and justice. In the absence of an adequate response, millions of people are left with no choice but to flee, primarily into neighbouring states; 85 per cent of the world's refugees remain in the Global South.

These dynamics and shortcomings not only generate refugee flows, but also make the resolution of refugee situations problematic and difficult to achieve. The refugee regime does not have the authority to address these root causes of conflict and inequality. Instead, it relies on other actors within the international community: the UN Security Council, development actors, and regional organizations. In the absence of an effective response to the drivers of displacement, refugee situations remain unresolved. The average duration of a refugee situation is now twenty years.

No two refugee situations will be the same, and there is no one way to resolve all forms of forced migration. Instead, responses need to be tailored to address both the experience of exile and the root causes of displacement. So long as root causes remain unaddressed, the cycle of displacement may continue.

Intolerance

Most contemporary refugee movements and internal displacements are no longer caused by ideological conflict between states, as they were during the Cold War. Instead, most are now the consequence of ethnic, communal, and religious conflicts as well as violence and nationality disputes and intolerance. Virtually all refugee-producing conflicts taking place around the world are within states rather than between them. Very few modern states are ethnically homogeneous as approximately 5,000 ethnic groups and over 8,000 languages exist in the world today. Ethiopia alone, with a population of 105 million people, is home to more than eighty ethnic groups. Some of the larger ethnic minorities in Ethiopia have tried to create ethnically pure enclaves by driving minorities from their homes. For example, about 1.4 million of the smaller ethnic groups have been driven from their home territories in recent years.

In most countries today, ethnic, religious, and cultural antagonisms between different groups of people such as between Rohingya Muslims and Burmese Buddhists in Myanmar, Hutus and Tutsis in Burundi and Rwanda, Tamils and Sinhalese in Sri Lanka, between Sunnis and Shia Muslims across much of the Middle East, and between Christians and Jews and Muslims illustrate the local roots of many atrocities and refugee exoduses. In recent times, individuals supporting white supremacy have killed and injured Mexican migrants in Texas and Ohio, Jews in synagogues in Maryland, Muslims in mosques in New Zealand and Sri Lanka, and in numerous other locations. In China, religious and ethnic minorities such as the Uyghur Muslim population in Xinjiang province, Buddhists in Tibet, and other ethnic and religious minorities, are persecuted and subjected to mass internment and persecution at the hands of intolerant and hostile Chinese communist authorities.

The changing nature of conflict

Refugee situations are also frequently the consequence of contemporary conflicts which last a very long time and are extremely difficult to resolve. During the Cold War, refugee camps in Pakistan, Honduras, Thailand, and Cambodia were the base of so-called 'refugee warriors' who were armed by either the United States, the Soviet Union, or the host communities. These were long-standing conflicts, which generated huge numbers of refugees, many of whom remain in exile today.

With the end of the Cold War, new conflicts emerged in many regions of the Global South, leading to millions more refugees. In the absence of effective peacebuilding in Somali, Sudan,

Afghanistan, and elsewhere, these refugees continue to live in exile today. Most refugees and IDPs today are confronted with unending exile entailing a sequence of moves from one place to another or being stuck in the limbo of overcrowded refugee camps or urban slums, mostly in the Global South.

Even contemporary conflicts are long-standing and protracted. The war in Syria, for example, has raged for over nine years and by the end of 2019 more than 6.6 million people had fled the country while millions more were internally displaced. Protracted refugee situations also exist in Afghanistan, Yemen, South Sudan, and the Democratic Republic of the Congo (DRC), among many other countries. Some refugee groups, like the Rohingya, have been forcibly, brutally, and repeatedly driven from their home villages in Rhakine state in Myanmar in successive mass exoduses to neighbouring Bangladesh and countries in South and Southeast Asia in the 1970s, 1990s, and recently in 2017.

Many people would have heard of the Rohingyas, Syrians, and Congolese, but what of the Sahrawi? In 1975, the Sahrawi refugees were forcibly expelled from their original homes when Moroccan military forces defeated the Sahrawi Polisario Front and annexed the Western Sahara. Since then, Morocco has controlled more than two-thirds of the Western Sahara and has suppressed any attempt by the Polisario Front to establish an independent government. As a result, tens of thousands of Sahrawi refugees remain in exile, the majority of whom reside in refugee camps in Tindouf, Algeria, and in Mauritania.

A number of new developments and trends in warfare have further contributed to the growing speed and scale of forced displacements in recent years. Hybrid warfare is a military strategy that employs political warfare and blends conventional warfare, irregular warfare, and cyber-attacks with other strategies such as fake news, diplomacy, intervention in foreign elections, and malicious state behaviour including murder and poisoning opponents.

Misinformation

In recent years media companies, in particular, have expanded their reach and influence across the globe. In many situations, extreme nationalist and populist leaders and their supporters misuse social media to influence public opinion, sway elections, exacerbate conflicts, provoke discord, and promote violence and hatred towards ethnic and religious minorities and political opponents. Fake news and doctored photographs and film clips provoke hatred and fear and incite people to attack and expel minorities in countries with strong ethnic or religious differences, such as Myanmar and Sri Lanka, to name only a couple of examples.

Technology companies play a significant role in fomenting political extremism. Digital disinformation, lies, and doctored photos are flagrantly and routinely used today on the messaging platforms of social media such as Facebook, Twitter, Instagram, YouTube, and others to spread disinformation and prejudice online, to influence public opinion and promote hatred of ethnic minorities and religious groups, and for other malign purposes.

Along with increased hate speech, deliberate misinformation, and misuse of social media, local forms of violence and warfare have emerged, particularly in collapsing states where competing warlords, criminal and youth gangs, and terrorist organizations destroy entire religious, historical, social, economic, and political systems in their fight to promote their causes and to achieve access to ever scarcer resources.

Technologies of war

In addition, the growth of the worldwide market for small arms and landmines has made internal wars more violent and more frequent. Consequently, conflicts today not only last longer but often kill and displace more people than in the recent past.

Most significantly, mass expulsions of refugees are now regularly used as weapons of war. Kelly Greenhill has written that governments and their opponents use population displacements for a variety of political and military purposes. Such strategies help armed groups gain or maintain control over people, territory, and other resources. They can be used to establish culturally or ethnically homogeneous societies, to perpetuate the dominance of one group over another, to provide a means of removing groups of people whose loyalty to the state or official religion is questionable. Finally, in recent conflicts, refugees are even used as human shields to protect rebel military forces from attack in times of conflict. Thus, in many situations, population displacement has become the very objective of wars.

In recent years, displacement and human suffering have been compounded by the increasing widespread use of siege warfare, particularly in the Middle East but increasingly in other parts of the world as well.

Since 2011, Syrian government forces, along with their Russian and Iranian allies, have bombed major Syrian cities with intense military attacks using cluster bombs, incendiary devices, and chemical weapons to kill and disable civilians including women and children. Civilian areas and populations have been indiscriminately targeted in order to force the surrender of the Assad regime's military and civilian opposition. Besieged communities are typically surrounded by armed actors who restrict the movement of essential goods and people in and out of the areas under siege. Despite numerous UN Security Council resolutions calling for immediate humanitarian access to civilian populations in such situations, the UN and other humanitarian organizations are routinely refused entry to the areas under attack. At the same time, hospitals' medical staff, schools, and public areas are deliberately and systematically targeted by military forces from the air and on the ground. In the attempt to deny the resistance their most immediate needs, the movement of civilians and delivery of goods, including essential medical supplies, are prohibited in most besieged areas.

In Yemen, Saudi and United Arab Republic forces have employed tactics similar to those used in Syria, including indiscriminate air attacks and embargos of essential food and medical supplies to try to defeat Houthi rebels and their Iranian supporters. Besieged areas are surrounded by armed actors who restrict the movement of essential goods and people in and out of the area. Starving and emaciated children are denied food and medical care in what is widely perceived to be one of the world's biggest contemporary humanitarian disasters.

Complex emergencies

The majority of today's refugee crises are also so-called complex emergencies, combining political instability, ethnic and religious tensions, armed conflicts, economic collapse, environmental degradation, and the disintegration of civil society. Refugee movements frequently spill over borders to neighbouring countries and aggravate existing problems, such as environmental damage or severe food shortages. Refugee emergencies have recently affected entire regions, such as the Great Lakes region in Central Africa, the Horn of Africa, North Africa and the Maghreb, the Middle East, parts of South and Central America, and Southwest Asia. In recent years, few of these conflicts and refugee crises have been fully resolved and the number of long-lasting or protracted refugee situations has spiralled out of control. By 2019, about two-thirds of the world's refugees had been in prolonged exile for more than five years.

Wars in other countries such as the Democratic Republic of the Congo, Central African Republic, Syria, and Afghanistan are also lasting longer than before as new power structures, parallel economies, and increasing numbers of armed factions are created within these war societies, making the settlement of conflicts extremely difficult. With the absence of formal military authority in many of these countries, combatants tend to mobilize around loyalties and allegiances which have as much to do with personal survival and personal enrichment as with any political or ideological agenda. Those possessing power are almost invariably opposed to the settlement of crises as such initiatives endanger and erode their power base and access to valuable resources, such as diamonds, gold, coltan, and other precious metals which they routinely loot and sell for huge sums in international markets. These funds are used to finance armed gangs and militias. In countries like the Democratic Republic of the Congo, armed factions are able to use their profits from the sale of precious metals to purchase arms and to rampage, rape, and displace local citizens with virtual impunity. Similarly, in the Middle East and North Africa, non-government militias use the control of oil resources to finance war and terror.

The return of famine

After several decades of declining numbers of famines around the world, new grave situations of starvation and mass hunger have returned, producing growing numbers of refugees and IDPs.

During recent conflicts, food and medical supplies have assumed great strategic significance. Consequently, food distribution centres and medical facilities and hospitals in Syria, Yemen, and other countries have been specifically targeted and regularly bombed. These policies amount to de facto depopulation programmes through enforced famine or expulsion of civilian populations in areas of pressing need.

In response to these crises, UNHCR and aid agencies have to operate in areas where even the most humanitarian activities are perceived as a factor affecting the outcome of the confrontation. For example, throughout most of the fighting in Afghanistan and Yemen in recent years, governments and international agencies have provided considerable food and medical assistance both bilaterally and through UN agencies such as the World Food Programme, UNICEF, the World Health Organization, and UNHCR. Along with UN assistance, non-governmental organizations (NGOs) such as Médecins sans Frontières (MSF), CARE, Oxfam, Mercy Corps, Save the Children, and thousands of others provide emergency aid and often work in areas which are besieged and insecure.

Despite these efforts, the UN and intergovernmental agencies, NGOs, and governments active in providing refugee and humanitarian relief aid often struggle to obtain adequate funds to carry out their work. The political and security considerations and priorities guiding donor government and international agency decisions regarding humanitarian access and delivery of assistance seriously compromise the equitable distribution of humanitarian aid. Thus, in many instances, humanitarian work is not only a perilous activity for the UN and other aid agencies but is also insufficient for many uprooted and persecuted people in danger of starvation.

Genocide, politicide, and other international war crimes

At the close of the Second World War, and while the memory of the Holocaust and other atrocities were fresh in their minds, UN member states declared that 'never again' would the crime of genocide be tolerated by the international community. Nevertheless, despite the passage in December 1948 of both the UN Convention on the Prevention and Punishment of the Crime of Genocide and the UN Universal Declaration of Human Rights, the international community still fails to prevent such crimes today.

In addition to the crime of genocide, politicide is the deliberate physical destruction of a group whose members share the main characteristic of belonging to a specific political movement. It is a type of political repression, and one means of the political cleansing of populations, with another being forced migration. During the past seventy years, there have been numerous instances of genocide and politicide which the international community has failed to prevent, or to punish those responsible. To list only a few of the most grievous of these mass killings during the past fifty years: in 1972 a Tutsi government in Burundi murdered hundreds of thousands of Hutus; during the same period the Khmer Rouge in Cambodia murdered 1.5 million Cambodians; in the 1980s the Guatemalan military killed over 50,000 Mayan nationals and Saddam Hussein's forces murdered some 100,000 Kurds in Iraq; in 1994, Rwandan Hutus slaughtered over half a million of their Tutsi neighbours while the world and a UN force in Rwanda stood by. Similarly, in 1995 in Srebrenica in the former Yugoslavia, UN peacekeeping troops did not intervene as hundreds of Bosnian men and boys were executed by Serbian soldiers. In the early 21st century ethnic groups in Darfur were slaughtered at the command of Sudan's former President Omar al-Bashir.

Moreover, despite the recent establishment of the International Criminal Court and the adoption of a UN resolution on the 'Responsibility to Protect', incidents of genocide have repeatedly occurred. For decades, the military and Buddhist radicals in Myanmar have stigmatized and targeted the Muslim Rohingya as well as the Shan, Kachin, Karen, Karenni, Chin, and other ethnic and religious minorities along the borders with Thailand, China, and India. Similar atrocities and genocides have recently occurred in South Sudan, the Central African Republic, the Democratic Republic of the Congo, Sri Lanka, and elsewhere in the developing world. In an effort to kill and erase from existence the Yazidi Christian community in Iraq, Isis forces attacked and murdered Yazidi men, kidnapped their children, and forced women and girls to become sex slaves. In Nigeria Boko Haram carried out similar kidnappings and killings, again without meaningful international response.

Conclusion

These incidents of persecution on the basis of religion and ethnic differences, engineered displacement, mass killings, and kidnappings have occurred without sufficient international response. The UN Security Council, whose responsibility it is to enforce breaches of international law in such situations, has often been inactive and sharply divided over such matters. In the absence of efforts on the part of the United Nations, regional organizations, and governments to prevent genocide and punish perpetrators, genocides and mass killings will continue to be a major source and cause of future refugee movements.

While the specific causes of forced displacement are diverse, they share a common characteristic of being rooted in political interests. Until the international community is able to effectively and reliably address these root causes, forced displacement will remain a common feature of world affairs. As such, it is critical to ensure that international responses to forced migration are effective in ensuring protection for refugees and providing for their well-being, while also laying the foundation for refugees to find a solution to their plight.

Chapter 4
Responding to refugee movements

When governments created a system for responding to the needs of refugees, they agreed on the principles and institutions necessary to provide protection for refugees and to find a solution to their plight. As discussed in Chapter 2, the fundamental principles are detailed in the 1951 Refugee Convention. The core institution of the system is UNHCR. Together, these instruments are supposed to ensure that refugees have access to key rights while they are in exile. They are also supposed to help refugees find a solution to their plight.

Because refugees are individuals who have fled their home country and no longer enjoy the protection afforded to citizens of a state, the 1951 Refugee Convention also sets out the rights to which all refugees are entitled, namely that refugees should have access to national courts, the right to employment and education, and to a host of other social, economic, and civil rights on a par with nationals of the host country. UNHCR also has responsibility for monitoring and supporting states' compliance with these rights. As we saw in Chapter 2, UNHCR has a long history of protecting and assisting millions of refugees and other displaced people around the world. For decades, the international structure for the protection of refugees provided a global treaty framework which (with some major exceptions) assisted and protected many refugees in Europe, Africa, Latin America, and most of Asia and North America.

Since its creation in December 1950 by the UN General Assembly, UNHCR has had a specific mandate, namely to ensure that refugees have access to protection from persecution. The framers of the UNHCR mandate also set out a range of 'durable solutions' aimed at resolving refugee problems. These solutions include resettlement in another country, local integration in a nearby receiving country, or repatriation to their home countries when conditions are safe enough for refugees to return and reclaim their rights in their country of origin.

However, the global refugee system is not able to do this work on its own. Instead, every element of the system was designed around the understanding that governments would cooperate with the regime and each other to make the system work. UNHCR's 1950 statute does not give the organization the authority to work on its own. Instead, it works under the authority of the UN General Assembly, which is made up of states. UNHCR cannot provide solutions for refugees on its own. Instead, it is mandated to assist governments in finding solutions and can only implement solutions with the approval and cooperation of governments.

The entire logic of the global refugee system is premised on the cooperation of states. In fact, the preamble of the 1951 Convention notes that 'the granting of asylum can place unduly heavy burdens on certain countries', that the issue of refugees is 'international in scope and nature', and that protection and solutions for refugees 'cannot be achieved without international cooperation'.

While states have reaffirmed their commitment to the idea of international cooperation dozens of times over the past seventy years through UN General Assembly resolutions and other statements, there remains no binding obligation for them to cooperate and to ensure predictable, equitable, and effective international action in response to the needs of refugees. In fact, today's global refugee system has often had difficulty in providing both adequate protection and assistance for refugees and greater stability for refugees in sending and receiving states. While countries to which refugees apply for asylum are obliged to receive refugees and not to forcibly return them to a country where they fear persecution (the principle of non-refoulement—as discussed in Chapter 1), there is no binding obligation on states to share the costs associated with the provision of asylum. In recent years, millions of refugees have been denied many of their basic rights, including freedom of movement. Instead, closed borders, massive concrete walls, razor wire and electric fences, as well as armed border police and military forces, are now regularly used throughout the world to keep out refugees and asylum seekers. Increasing numbers of states are also forcibly returning refugees to dangerous situations in violation of international law.

The failure of the international community to provide effective responses to refugee movements and to uphold the principles outlined in the UNHCR mandate and the 1951 Refugee Convention are also contributing to the recent growth of populist politicians and extremist right-wing parties in many regions of the world. For many such groups, refugees and asylum seekers are perceived as evidence of the dangers of globalization and open societies. Xenophobia, widespread racism and intolerance of religious, ethnic, trans-sexual, and other minority groups have spread and have incited numerous massacres and refugee exoduses across the globe.

This chapter discusses the principal constraints on responding to refugee movements through international cooperation within the context of a radically changing international political system, an expanding global mobility regime, and a growing and diverse group of displaced people in need of assistance and protection. Finally, the chapter will briefly address some of the key issues and problems the global refugee system is likely to face in the future.

A changing global order and shifting
state interests

When states created the global refugee system at the end of the
Second World War, there was near consensus on the need for a
collective response. Over the past seventy years, however, a rapidly
changing global order and shifting state interests have eroded that
consensus. This has meant that UNHCR, as the key institution of
the global refugee system, has been left to try to generate
cooperation and support from increasingly reluctant and
restrictive states. Moreover, while UNHCR has often
demonstrated its ability to act independently during the past
seventy years, its activities and evolution have been defined and, at
times, constrained by global politics and the influence and
interests of powerful states. The organization is almost entirely
dependent on voluntary contributions (almost entirely from
states) to carry out its work. This gives significant influence to a
limited number of donor states in the Global North who have
traditionally funded the bulk of UNHCR's operational budget, as
discussed below.

At the same time, UNHCR works at the invitation of states
hosting refugees to undertake activities on their territories and
must therefore negotiate with a range of host governments,
especially in the Global South. UNHCR is consequently placed in
the difficult position of trying to facilitate cooperation between
donor states in the Global North and refugee-hosting states in the
Global South who host 85 per cent of the world's refugees.

Most significantly, UNHCR works within changing political and
global contexts, with shifting dynamics of displacement, and with
a range of partners, both within and outside the UN System. The
humanitarian world is now commonly characterized as a
'competitive marketplace' which involves a vast range of actors
each with their own mandate, institutional identity, and drive to

protect their own interests. These political and institutional constraints often affect the functioning of the global refugee regime and the ability of UNHCR to fulfil its mandate.

While UNHCR frequently finds itself caught between the human rights principles that underpin the global refugee regime and the competing political, security, and economic interests of states and other actors, these dynamics are further influenced by changes in world politics and the global order. For example, the end of the Cold War in the late 1980s not only presented UNHCR with an unprecedented opportunity to resolve some of the world's longest-standing refugee situations, such as in Southeast Asia and Central America, through large-scale resettlement and repatriation programmes but also presented new challenges to the organization. In the 1990s, the international community was confronted with a number of new intrastate conflicts and refugee crises, including the collapse of Somalia, the break-up of the former Yugoslavia, the mass exodus from Kosovo, and genocide in Rwanda. Each of these crises witnessed significant and complex dynamics of forced displacement for which UNHCR was called upon to provide humanitarian assistance. However, in many cases, governments used humanitarian relief as a substitute for political action to address the root causes of mass displacement.

It has become increasingly difficult for UNHCR to persuade states to host refugees and to offer asylum. In the Global North, refugee policy and practice have been marked by a shift from asylum to containment where Western states have largely limited the asylum they offer to refugees and have focused on efforts to contain refugees to their region of origin. These measures include non-arrival policies, such as airline carrier sanctions and visa requirements, diversion policies, such as sending refugees to so-called 'safe third countries' as a means to avoid an influx of asylum seekers into their own territories, and interdiction at sea policies which prevent boatloads of refugees from arriving in potential asylum countries such as in Europe and return them to their regions of origin in Africa, the Middle East, and elsewhere.

To further this objective, many Western states have adopted an increasingly restrictive application of the 1951 Convention for asylum applicants. A range of deterrent policies, such as forced separation of families, the prolonged detention of asylum seekers, and the denial of social assistance to asylum applicants, are now common practice in the United States, the European Union, and Australia, among other states.

These developments have placed a significant strain on asylum countries in the Global South, which continue to host the great majority of the world's refugees. In recent years, taking their cue from states in the Global North, the developing world also began to place restrictions on displaced people seeking asylum. Some states have closed their borders to prevent arrivals, pushed for the early and often unsustainable return of refugees to their country of origin, and, in exceptional cases, forcibly expelled entire refugee populations.

More generally, states nearly everywhere have been placing limits on the quality of asylum they offer to refugees, by denying them the social and economic rights contained in the 1951 Convention, such as freedom of movement and the right to seek employment. Many states in the South either detain asylum seekers and returnees in overcrowded and often dangerous detention centres, such as those in Libya and Tunisia, or require refugees to remain in isolated and insecure refugee camps for protracted periods, cut off from the local community, and fully dependent on international assistance. Millions more refugees are stranded in sprawling urban areas with limited or often no assistance and limited livelihood opportunities. As a result of their reliance on the informal economy and day wages, millions of refugees around the world were among the most significantly affected as states implemented lockdown policies to prevent the spread of COVID-19 in early 2020.

The crises of asylum in both the North and South have confronted UNHCR with a nearly impossible task. While mandated by the international community to ensure the protection of refugees and find solutions to their plight, UNHCR cannot fulfil this task without the financial and political support and cooperation of states. In recent decades, states have sometimes excluded UNHCR from refugee responses and increasingly devised their own responses to insulate themselves from the growing number of refugees seeking access to their territories.

This lack of cooperation by states, coupled with a global impasse over cooperation between Northern donor countries and Southern host states, has significantly frustrated the ability of the global refugee system, including UNHCR, to assist and protect refugees in recent years. To understand how cooperation can be encouraged, it is important to understand the relationship between UNHCR, the UN System, and UN Member States, and how these relationships have been leveraged to support cooperative refugee responses.

The UN System and international cooperation

While UNHCR has been reliant on states to do its work, states have also approved the gradual expansion of the scope of UNHCR's work. When UNHCR was created in 1950, there were just sixty UN Member States. Today, there are 193. As states in the Global South became independent from colonial rule through the 1960s, UN membership became an important marker of their independence. This also meant the majority of states in the UN General Assembly became states in the Global South, which also hosted the majority of the world's refugees. States in the Global South used this majority in two key ways. First, they passed resolutions calling for collective action in response to refugee situations in Southeast Asia, Central America, and Africa in the 1970s and 1980s. Second, they approved the gradual expansion of UNHCR to include the provision of international assistance, administration of refugee camps, working with new categories of forced migrants, and working in new geographic contexts. In fact, UNHCR turned repeatedly to the UN General Assembly throughout its early history to authorize the organization's involvement in emerging refugee situations in Africa and Asia.

More recently, the UN General Assembly played a central role in developing a new agreement on international cooperation for refugees and migrants. In response to the chaotic response to the arrival of some 1 million refugees and migrants in Europe in 2015, and in recognition of the failings of the current system globally, the UN Secretary-General and the President of the UN General Assembly launched a process to develop a more reliable response. The UN Secretary-General issued a report in April 2016 calling for greater international cooperation and solidarity to implement existing agreements, including the 1951 Convention. In September 2016, the UN General Assembly unanimously adopted the New York Declaration, outlining new commitments to collective action in responding to refugee movements and realizing refugee rights.

The 2016 New York Declaration also included a Comprehensive Refugee Response Framework (CRRF). The CRRF is a new approach to responding to refugee movements through cooperation and partnership. It is designed to include refugees themselves in creating solutions to allow refugees to be self-reliant and contribute to local economies. It also recognizes that refugees can make important contributions to their host communities, and that more effective responses will both build on the skills refugees bring while also addressing the costs associated with granting asylum. From 2016 to 2018, the CRRF was piloted in a dozen countries in the Global South and refugees were able to make important and lasting contributions.

On the basis of the experience of the CRRF, UNHCR led a series of consultations in 2017 and 2018 to develop a new Global Compact on Refugees (GCR). The vast majority of UNHCR

Member States affirmed the GCR in December 2018, with only Hungary and the United States voting against it. The GCR includes new mechanisms to respond to refugees, plans for regular global meetings to leverage commitments for refugees, and makes the participation of refugees themselves central in the development of new approaches. Only time will tell how significant the GCR will be in promoting international cooperation, but the process does show that states can cooperate when they are motivated to do so.

Governing the refugee regime

Despite these recent important developments, a critical problem today is the widespread perception within the UN System that refugees are UNHCR's 'problem', not a shared responsibility. This perception, likely a result of the territoriality and competition between UN agencies and the desire by states to insulate themselves from hosting refugees, has often resulted in the reluctance of other UN agencies to more fully engage in refugee issues and has frustrated recent efforts to articulate a more comprehensive and holistic engagement at the UN level in issues relating to refugees.

Another problem relates to limitations in the governance of the refugee regime. In 1958, several years after the creation of UNHCR, the UN General Assembly established the Executive Committee of the Programme of the United Nations High Commissioner for Refugees (ExCom). ExCom is responsible for approving the Office's annual budget and programme, for setting standards and reaching conclusions on international refugee protection policy issues, and for providing guidance on UNHCR's management, objectives, and priorities. It is the only specialized multilateral forum at the global level responsible for contributing to the development of international standards relating to refugee protection. In recent years, ExCom has become too large and politicized and it is frequently not an effective decision-making body. From an initial group of twenty-five members in the late 1950s, ExCom has grown along with the growth in membership of the UN General Assembly and now includes 106 Member States. Not only are there too many participants, but the issues are complex, divisive, and numerous and meetings are seldom a forum for organizational guidance as they once were. In addition, the increasing divide in interests between representatives from industrialized states and developing countries makes international consensus on refugee matters exceedingly difficult to achieve.

Given the shortcomings of ExCom as an authoritative decision-making body, individual donor governments and some key host states have come to establish the priorities that guide UNHCR's programme. In the early years of the organization, when its work was primarily focused on legal protection in Europe, UNHCR operated on a very modest budget. It was not until the global expansion of the Office in the late 1970s and 1980s that UNHCR's budget began to increase dramatically. Contributions from the UN Regular Budget now account for less than 3 per cent of UNHCR's Annual Budget of several billion dollars. In 2019, for example, UNHCR's Annual Budget was US$8.6 billion.

However, UNHCR's 1950 Statute makes it reliant on voluntary contributions for the vast majority of its work. There is no binding obligation on states to provide UNHCR with the funding it needs. Only the costs relating to the administrative functions of UNHCR are covered by the general budget of the UN. This means that all other activities, from the administration of refugee camps to the provision of legal assistance, are paid for by voluntary contributions from states, the private sector, and public donors. This dependence on voluntary contributions is compounded by the fact that around 80 per cent of the Office's budget comes from its top ten donor states, all of whom are rich, industrialized countries (Figure 2). In 2019, for example, the United States, European states, and Japan together accounted for almost two-thirds of funding to UNHCR.

Refugees

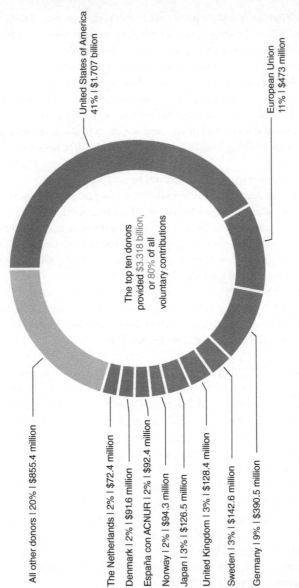

United States of America
41% | $1.707 billion

European Union
11% | $473 million

The top ten donors provided $3.318 billion, or 80% of all voluntary contributions

All other donors | 20% | $855.4 million

The Netherlands | 2% | $72.4 million

Denmark | 2% | $91.6 million

España con ACNUR | 2% | $92.4 million

Norway | 2% | $94.3 million

Japan | 3% | $126.5 million

United Kingdom | 3% | $128.4 million

Sweden | 3% | $142.6 million

Germany | 9% | $390.5 million

2. **Top ten donors to UNHCR, 2019.**

The unpredictability of funding and the geographic concentration of donors have placed UNHCR in a precarious political position. While the organization has attempted to safeguard the integrity of its mandate by being seen to be politically impartial, its ability to carry out its programmes continues to depend upon its ability to respond to the interests of a relatively small number of donor states.

The influence of donor states is further increased through their ability to specify how, where, and on what basis their contributions may be used by UNHCR. This practice, known as 'earmarking', remains commonplace. Typically, a certain percentage of contributions to UNHCR in any given year are 'tightly earmarked' for specific countries and activities, while another percentage are 'softly earmarked' for specific geographical regions and only a relatively small percentage come with no restrictions (Figure 3).

The United States, still the largest donor to UNHCR and accounting for more than a third of contributions to the organization, earmarks every dollar it gives to UNHCR. The practice of earmarking allows donors to exercise considerable influence over the work of UNHCR as programmes considered important by donors receive substantial support, while those deemed less important receive less support and sometimes nothing at all. For example, today donor governments still give vastly disproportionate amounts of aid to a few well-known crises, such as in Syria and Afghanistan, and far smaller amounts of aid to dozens of other refugee programmes, particularly in Africa.

The fact that donors largely contribute to UNHCR on the basis of their own perceived interests makes the concentration of donors all the more problematic. In 2019, the top ten donors were the major industrialized states, with all other countries accounting for less than a quarter of contributions to UNHCR. As a result, the interests of a relatively small number of Northern states have been highly influential in determining UNHCR's activities and policies.

Refugees

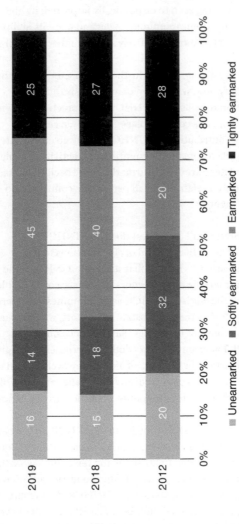

2019	16	14		45			25			
2018	15	18		40			27			
2012	20		32		20		28			

0% 10% 20% 30% 40% 50% 60% 70% 80% 90% 100%

■ Unearmarked ■ Softly earmarked ■ Earmarked ■ Tightly earmarked

3. Earmarking of contributions to UNHCR.

The significant role played by a small number of donors places UNHCR in a challenging political position. Perhaps the most damaging effect of a concentration of donors is the perception by Southern states that UNHCR is beholden to Northern donors and therefore is tied to their interests. These perceptions have further frustrated efforts at ensuring international cooperation within the global refugee regime. Reconciling the need to have an autonomous influence on states and supervising the refugee regime with being responsive to donor interests is a difficult balancing act for UNHCR.

There is also no binding obligation on states to provide solutions for refugees. While the 1951 Convention calls on states to naturalize refugees, states insist that the granting of citizenship is a sovereign act. The resettlement of refugees is also at the discretion of states. In 2019, for example, UNHCR reported that 1.4 million refugees were in need of resettlement, most on an urgent basis. But only twenty countries have regular resettlement programmes and decide which refugees to resettle and how many. The result is a significant gap between the level of need and the number resettled. In 2019, a total of 107,800 refugees were resettled by 26 countries. This represented a significant drop from 2016 when 163,206 refugees were resettled, mostly in the United States, Canada, and Australia. The drop in numbers for refugee resettlement is explained primarily by the significant decline in the US resettlement programme under the Trump administration. Resettlement efforts were further constrained in early 2020 due to a virtual suspension of international travel as a result of the global COVID-19 pandemic.

The refugee regime complex

The work of UNHCR has been further complicated by the dramatic increase in new forms of international cooperation at the bilateral, regional, and international levels in the areas of labour migration, international travel, human rights, humanitarianism, security, development, and peacebuilding. As noted by Alexander Betts, a 'refugee regime complex' has emerged in which these different institutions overlap, exist in parallel to each other, and influence states' policies towards refugees. The refugee regime complex has both positive and negative implications for the global refugee system and for the protection of refugees.

Many of the new institutions offer states the opportunity to bypass the global refugee system when responding to refugee movements. For example, new forms of interstate cooperation to stop irregular migration enable many states to limit the access of asylum seekers to their territories. Regional interstate forums have been established which enable governments to develop bilateral agreements on issues such as visa control, readmission agreements, international zones at airports, and extra-territorial border management. The European Union border control agency FRONTEX has a mandate to intercept asylum seekers and migrants in the Mediterranean before they reach European shores to make asylum claims. Since the arrival of over a million asylum seekers into Europe during 2015, the numbers of new arrivals by sea have dwindled to much lower levels as most boats are now seized before they reach Europe's shores and returned to Libya and other countries in the Middle East and North and West Africa.

The growth of the refugee complex has also meant that UNHCR must compete with other humanitarian actors for funds, visibility, and territory. Not surprisingly, UNHCR has spoken of an emerging 'humanitarian marketplace' within which the Office faces growing competition from other humanitarian service providers.

While competition has clearly complicated UNHCR's work and effectiveness, and while UNHCR has made some controversial decisions as a result of its desire to be seen as relevant to states, the emergence of overlapping institutions has also enabled the organization to develop new partnerships that permit it to better fulfil its mandate. For example, a number of international human rights instruments provide sources of refugee protection for refugees fleeing persecution that comes from outside of international refugee law—such as the example of individuals fleeing the consequences of climate change, as discussed in Chapter 1. At times, UNHCR has also collaborated with other UN institutions such as the United Nations Development Programme (UNDP), the World Bank, or IOM in ways that have enabled it to engage with the development and migration implications of forced displacement. In the future, UNHCR will likely have to further expand its international links by establishing stronger complementary overlap with other institutions such as the Office of the High Commissioner for Human Rights, the UN Peacebuilding Commission, and others.

Changing trends in forced migration

The increasingly diverse drivers of displacement, as outlined in Chapter 3, also make cooperation more difficult. Today, the global refugee system faces the most rapid period of change in the nature of forced displacement in the seven decades of its existence. New wars, protracted refugee situations, siege warfare, the return of the use of famine as a weapon of war, and a divided and largely ineffective UN Security Council have helped to produce the largest numbers of refugees and IDPs since the Second World War.

In addition to its work with refugees and asylum seekers, since 2005 UNHCR has assumed the lead role in ensuring host governments protect IDPs in conflict situations across the world. Moreover, climate change, state fragility, food insecurity, rapid urbanization, and regional and global terrorism all raise fundamental questions for new understandings of the limits of the global refugee system and UNHCR's ability to provide protection for the increasing populations displaced by these new developments.

Most significantly, international migration has increased rapidly in recent decades. UNHCR now works in a context in which the differences between refugees, asylum seekers, and migrants are often increasingly hard to distinguish. All these groups move for a variety of reasons including persecution, escape from violence, human rights violations, as well as in the search for employment and a better and safer standard of living for themselves and their families. Asylum seekers and migrants often use the same migration routes and states often fail to differentiate between them. Thus, mixed migration poses a huge challenge for the global refugee system. New sources of forced displacement such as climate change and environmental disasters are among the growing number of new threats to world order Moreover, as new drivers of cross-border displacement continue to emerge with the complex interaction of state fragility, environmental change across the globe, and food insecurity, the Office faces the dilemma of how to respond to other categories of vulnerable migrants who have protection needs.

As new challenges emerge in the future, the global refugee system and UNHCR will face the question of how to adapt and how to define the boundaries of its 'population of concern'. It will need to judiciously decide when and when not to take on new activities and functions. And when new challenges are recognized as requiring an international response, it will need to carefully judge whether to take on such tasks or to encourage other actors to assume responsibility.

While UNHCR remains the core institution of the global refugee system, the nature of displacement is fundamentally changing. As noted in Chapter 1, UNHCR has moved beyond its original focus on refugees to an involvement with other groups of displaced people. UNHCR's work and policy concerns are interconnected in complex ways with broader issue-areas such as migration, security, human rights, the environment, development, and peacebuilding. In order to fulfil its core mandate of achieving protection and solutions for refugees, UNHCR cannot avoid engaging proactively with these areas. However, UNHCR cannot infinitely expand its mandate and become a migration organization or a development organization. Rather, UNHCR should play a facilitative and catalytic role in mobilizing other actors to fulfil their responsibilities with respect to refugees.

UNHCR will also need to become more focused and strategic in the advocacy, coordination, and facilitation role that it plays. To be able to play such a role, UNHCR will need to overcome some key challenges—its own internal governance and accountability, its ability to secure un-earmarked funding from donors, and its ability to leverage solutions for refugees—while developing ways of engaging more effectively with the UN system, regional organizations, states and NGOs, and increasingly with refugees and other groups under their care.

Conclusion

The global refugee system has adapted and changed over time in order to balance the interests of states, the protection of refugees, and UNHCR's own institutional interests. International cooperation between states remains essential for refugees to find solutions. In the absence of reliable cooperation between states, and as states become more restrictive in their responses to refugees, UNHCR will continue to play an important role in mobilizing responses for refugees.

Given the importance of UNHCR, it may be encouraging that its history highlights the significant role that an international organization can play as the guardian of an institutional framework over time in spite of changing configurations of state interests and power relations. However, it also highlights how the tensions and contradictions implicit in this role can shape the trajectory of the organization itself and even affect its central role of the protection of refugees. It is only by confronting and responding effectively and creatively to these tensions and readjusting its structures and tactics that UNHCR will be able to fully realize its mandate of protecting refugees and finding solutions to their plight.

More fundamentally, however, the governance of the global refugee system shows that UNHCR alone cannot ensure protection and solutions for refugees. The system is premised on the understanding that states will cooperate to bring about solutions. While recent developments, such as the 2018 Global Compact on Refugees, demonstrate that states still recognize the need for cooperation, states are still not obligated to cooperate. Until cooperation becomes more reliable, effective, and predictable, the interests of states will continue to determine outcomes for refugees.

Chapter 5
Perceptions and misperceptions about refugees

The lived experiences of refugees and asylum seekers are often far removed from how they are represented in the media and public discourse. Refugees in flight have been violently and abruptly uprooted from everything familiar and important. They have left their homes and neighbourhoods, their families and friends, and their jobs. Their children's schools, their places of worship, their hospitals are often bombed and in ruin. They flee all this only to encounter a new reality as refugees and asylum seekers. Suddenly the only things that are important are trying to survive and to reach a safe place where they can seek ways to rebuild their lives.

The experience of flight and exile is as diverse and unique as the stories of the 26 million refugees in the world today. While it would be hard to generalize from these diverse experiences, the responses of states, the lack of international cooperation, and the limits of the global refugee system detailed in Chapter 4 have fuelled many misperceptions about refugees.

Where the global refugee system works, refugees can, and do, thrive. Where refugees enjoy their rights, they make significant contributions to their host communities and countries. Where refugees are given agency, they are key actors in finding solutions to their own plight. Restrictive policies affect all refugees, but can also compound the challenges faced by particular categories of

vulnerable refugees, such as unaccompanied children and refugees
with disabilities.

How are refugees (mis)represented?

Most refugees today are confronted with unending exile entailing
a protracted sequence of moves from one place to another or
being stuck for years in the limbo of overcrowded refugee camps,
urban ghettos, or detention centres. Even in protracted exile,
refugees who are allowed to be self-reliant can make important
contributions. However, as seen in Chapter 4, many governments
have placed deep restrictions on refugees and denied them the
chance to be self-reliant. These restrictions place refugees in
impossible situations, often leading to experiences of violence and
suffering, which compound their vulnerability. In their search for
refuge and protection, a growing number of refugees and forced
migrants also experience organized violence, including people
trafficking, kidnapping, slavery, extortion, and sexual violence.

Although the great majority of refugees in flight seek safety in
neighbouring countries in the Global South, some refugees travel
across continents to seek refuge and asylum in the Global North.
When they finally do reach a place of safety, they often face a
series of new challenges including discrimination and disbelief on
the part of receiving governments, the media, and local host
populations in the countries they flee to.

Immigration and refugee issues strike deep social, cultural,
religious, and political chords in many host countries, even those
with well-established traditions of immigration and openness to
refugees. The spontaneous arrival of large numbers of refugees,
asylum seekers, and migrants is frequently perceived as an
economic burden and cultural threat to the populations of
receiving countries. The host population will be on the watch for
any threat from refugees and immigrants to their own interests.
They will often resent any changes that these newcomers might

make to the political and social complexity and stability of their country, despite the many contributions that refugees can bring. Receiving societies might also resent the attention and assistance given the newcomers and fear that the influx of labour will drive down wages and create unemployment while driving up the cost of housing, food, and other goods.

Opposition to migration is a major feature of contemporary politics. In particular, for many Europeans, Americans, and Australians, the presence of growing Muslim communities in their countries raises key questions about nationality, religion, and cultural pluralism. Fear of Islamic fundamentalism and terrorism, increasing violence between migrants and local populations, and the growing popularity of extremist right-wing, anti-immigrant political parties are all impeding the assimilation of the millions of Muslim refugees, migrants, and guest-workers now living in the EU. In many Eastern European countries, particularly Hungary, the Czech Republic, and Poland, populism, neo-fascism, and other forms of extreme nationalism, xenophobia, and racism are growing and have the potential to impede democratization and provoke political instability. Even in Western Europe, far-right, anti-immigrant political parties are gaining support, particularly in Austria, the Netherlands, Italy, France, Germany, the UK, Sweden, and Denmark, among others.

In other parts of the world, migrants and refugees are also often perceived as a threat to the cultural identity of the receiving state and are used as grievances against ruling governments by their political opponents. In Pakistan, for example, opposition parties have claimed for a long time that their government has sold out the interest of the nation in their effort to provide long-term refuge to neighbouring Afghan refugees and have campaigned for their return to Afghanistan.

While anti-refugee voices have tended to prevail over pro-refugee groups in some receiving countries, support for accepting refugees remains strong among members and groups of civil society in many countries, including in North America, Europe, Australia, and New Zealand. Lawyers, human rights activists, local religious groups and congregations and refugee networks, international and national NGOs, such as Amnesty International, Human Rights Watch, and Médecins sans Frontières, and many local community groups advocate strongly for assisting and protecting refugees and asylum seekers.

Advocates for welcoming refugees point to the overwhelming evidence of the many contributions refugees make to their new societies when welcomed and allowed to integrate. Recent history includes prominent refugees in fields as diverse as science, art, business, sports, government, and academia. Within a year of arriving in Canada in 2016, for example, Syrian refugees had opened businesses that employed Canadians and refugees alike. Refugees resettled to Canada from Vietnam in the 1980s are now sponsoring Syrian refugees. A Canadian organization co-founded by refugees, Jumpstart Refugee Talent, is working to match the skills refugees have with Canadian employers looking for such skilled workers. And refugees have become powerful voices through groups like the Global Refugee-led Network in advocating for the rights of refugees and the benefit of including refugees in discussions around policy and practice.

When a mass influx of displaced people occurs, however, politicians in both sending and receiving countries are more likely to be concerned about the impact of this flow on their own power positions and on domestic stability within their societies. If the refugees and migrants are perceived to contribute to the receiving state's power base and economic and cultural stability, policymakers are more likely to accept and in some cases even welcome the newcomers. Historically, state officials have understood that the more incoming refugees have in common with the local population in racial, linguistic, religious, and cultural terms, the easier will be the complex task of integrating the refugee and immigrant population into the local community.

On the other hand, if the influx is perceived as a threat to the national stability and security of either the sending or receiving state, or if anti-refugee rhetoric is seen to bring political advantage, politicians will highlight the risks of forced population movements and evoke fears of interstate tension, domestic opposition, and even conflict. In response to perceived political benefits, many political leaders, particularly in the Global North, increasingly present migration as a threat to inter-communal harmony. Some claim that an influx of foreign nationals will threaten major societal values by altering the ethnic, cultural, religious, and linguistic composition of the host populations.

These restrictive, anti-refugee narratives from political leaders are not always shared across society and often compete with more sympathetic and humanitarian responses. Recent research by social anthropologists and other researchers shows that receiving societies initially often depict newly arriving refugees through particular narratives that characterize them as victims of tragedy and as people without agency and voice. For their part, the media often describe newly arriving refugees as traumatized, speechless, and bereft victims without agency, rather than as individuals with the potential to make important contributions to society and the economy.

These stereotypes around refugees also frequently inform understanding of forced migration across mainstream media, humanitarian action, and popular opinion. Many journalists, television reporters, and politicians commonly portray refugees in dramatic and mostly inaccurate terms such as 'streams' and 'floods' and 'waves' of humanity. In recent years, security fears concerning the threat of international terrorism have risen not only in Europe, US cities, and Australia but in New Zealand, Sri Lanka, and throughout the Middle East and parts of Africa.

Refugees and asylum seekers have been viewed and represented in dramatic terms as 'economic migrants in disguise', 'dangerous terrorists', or as 'carriers of infectious diseases'.

Anti-refugee rhetoric has recently been used for political gain by politicians in the United States, Australia, the UK, and many EU countries. For example, President Trump described people who are fleeing violence in Central America to seek asylum in America as 'animals' and claimed that Arab terrorists and violent criminals disguised as refugees are pouring into the United States. Fear-mongering of refugee and migrant inflows has increased everywhere. In Europe and Latin America, populist and right-wing political parties advocate similar anti-refugee and anti-immigrant policies. Given this political rhetoric, it should come as no surprise that a growing number of governments and citizens in the Global North are increasingly reluctant to bear the perceived domestic, economic, and security risks of admitting both refugees and asylum seekers.

How are asylum seekers treated by officials?

As we saw in Chapter 1, international law guarantees those fleeing persecution the right to request asylum in another country. Article 14 of the Universal Declaration of Human Rights clearly states that 'everyone has the right to seek and enjoy in other countries asylum from persecution'. In practice, however, the process is much more complicated and problematic. In most cases the authorities who review and assess asylum seekers' applications determine whether a person is a refugee on a case-by-case basis. Asylum seekers will be asked to prove that their claim to asylum and refugee status is genuine by demonstrating before a tribunal or court that they have a well-founded fear of persecution or risk death if they are forcibly returned to their home country. Usually, those persons who are found not to qualify for asylum as refugees are either deported to their country of origin or are given a temporary right to remain.

Seeking asylum is not a crime. Yet many asylum seekers across the world are regularly kept in detention holding centres while waiting to have their cases heard by immigration officers. Sometimes they are held indefinitely and in degrading conditions. Their medical and psychological needs are often ignored or downplayed. For many, detention is the precursor to their deportation back to the countries from which they have fled. Refugee and human rights organizations criticize these measures and policies as inhumane and unnecessary.

Conditions in many detention centres are unwelcoming or even punitive and have the objective of deterring others from seeking asylum. At times, asylum seekers are even kept in maximum-security prisons alongside convicted criminals. In Australia, asylum seekers have been held offshore for years in highly punitive conditions in holding centres on the nearby Pacific islands of Nauru and Manus. Over 80 per cent of the asylum seekers held there have developed mental health problems. Refugee children, in particular, have suffered under conditions of unending detention. In the United States, asylum-seeking families have been deliberately separated upon arrival in the country. Children as young as 12 months old have been taken from their parents as soon as the family arrives at the US border. Children are detained in separate facilities and warehoused, sometimes hundreds of miles away from their parents. In the UK, over 25,000 asylum seekers, including survivors of torture, are detained every year in one of ten detention centres across the country. Many applicants face long-drawn-out and traumatic legal processes. Those found not to be refugees are often forcibly deported to unsafe countries such as Somalia, Afghanistan, and the Democratic Republic of the Congo where armed groups, inter-communal violence, and other risks are rampant.

As the public and official discourse on refugees, asylum seekers, and migrants in receiving countries becomes more hostile and distorted, it is more difficult for displaced people to gain admission as refugees in traditional resettlement and asylum countries such as Australia, Europe, and North America. Many asylum seekers are perceived as untruthful and unreliable in testimony before adjudicators in national asylum tribunals and immigration hearings.

Disbelief of asylum seekers' traumatic accounts today is so great that increasingly asylum applicants need to be corroborated by more 'trustworthy voices' such as people with expert knowledge of the country they have fled from, as well as testimony from country and medical experts who can confirm the prevalence of torture or sexual violence. Victims of torture, rape, or other physical abuse may find it traumatizing and difficult to tell their story of persecution in court as it may be impossible for some individuals to recount the physical pain or memory of torture. This is particularly the case for those from cultures where such things are simply not spoken about.

Decisions on asylum rely heavily on the claimants' personal accounts and the way in which the claimants piece together and recollect the events that led to their forced departure. They are often required to testify in an official courtroom setting, which puts further pressure on them to recount their experiences as part of the process of assessing the genuineness and truthfulness of their asylum claims.

Increasing restrictionism

During 2014 and 2015, over a million refugees, asylum seekers, and migrants fleeing conflicts in Syria, Afghanistan, and Yemen, among other states, appeared on Europe's doorstep, in much greater numbers than in recent years. Instead of developing a comprehensive and rights-based response to these claims, opposition to further inflows of migrants and asylum seekers quickly grew among most EU states. Political inaction and the failure to cooperate turned a difficult situation into a crisis of mass proportions.

Anti-refugee and anti-migrant sentiment also commonly appeared among many of the world's newspapers and other media. There also occurred growing and widespread confusion concerning the distinctions between refugees, asylum seekers, migrants, and terrorists. Many politicians and other policymakers argued that refugees who are from different religious, linguistic, and ethnic backgrounds pose a danger to societal security and should be kept out of their countries. Both social and mass media increasingly characterized refugees and migrants as unwelcome newcomers who are either potential terrorists or are unwanted foreigners who will siphon resources away from 'real' citizens, take employment away from more qualified nationals, bring tensions from their home country with them, and commit a disproportionate amount of crime.

Refugee and asylum policies have become an even more contentious and divisive political issue in Western states in recent years. European governments have mobilized to resist the arrival of new flows by engaging in the interdiction on the Mediterranean of boatloads of refugees trying to reach European shores and forcibly repatriating new arrivals to their points of embarkation in the Middle East and Africa. The EU and national governments have also initiated new assistance programmes in countries and regions of refugee origin in Africa and the Middle East in an attempt to deter refugees from moving on to Europe. They have also undertaken military action to stem future flows of refugees trying to reach European shores. In the United States, the Trump administration sent military troops to the US–Mexico border to turn back new flows of refugees and forced migrants from Central America and Mexico and introduced several new restrictive admissions and detention policies for refugees, asylum seekers, and migrants. Similar use of force and long-term detention has characterized Australia's asylum policy in recent decades.

Vulnerable refugee groups

This trend of restrictionism compounds the vulnerability of many types of refugees. While refugees are people faced with impossible choices, and while many refugees are resilient, strong, courageous, and innovative, many also face particular vulnerabilities that the global refugee system finds hard to adequately address. The majority of refugees today are unaccompanied women and children who undertake perilous journeys in search of safety. Women, children and adolescents, the elderly, refugees with disabilities, and members of the LGBTQ community often face particular challenges during the experience of flight and exile.

For decades **refugee women** were the 'forgotten majority' in the international agendas of UNHCR, most governments, and many humanitarian organizations. It was widely held that the main threat to refugee women was their vulnerability to sexual violence. For example, during the 1992–5 war in Bosnia, between 20,000 and 50,000 mostly Bosnian Muslim women were brutally raped by Serbian military and police. More recently, Nigerian women have been kidnapped and mass raped by both Boko Haram and Nigerian security forces. In the Middle East Yazidi women were kidnapped and raped by Islamic State forces and in Southeast Asia Buddhist Myanmar soldiers gang-raped Muslim Rohingya women and committed other atrocities leading to a mass exodus of Rohingya to neighbouring Bangladesh.

UNHCR and some governments now give increasing recognition to women who have experienced persecution or suffered violence not only at the hands of military forces, police, or terrorist groups and other non-state actors, but also from family members. Gender-based persecution is now commonly recognized as grounds for being granted refugee status. In addition, female genital mutilation (FGM) is now considered a form of gender-based persecution. In recent years, UNHCR, many governments, and non-governmental refuge organizations have also introduced policies and guidelines designed to promote gender equality and the empowerment of women in camp settings, urban areas, and in other refugee contexts.

Children and adolescents are also often vulnerable as refugees. Over half of the world's refugees and internally displaced persons today are under 18 years of age. In conflicts across the world, children are being exposed to military attacks and brutal violence in their homes, schools, and playgrounds. Consequently, huge numbers of children have become refugees and displaced people. Entire generations of refugee children and teenagers are growing up without the support of family and community and with very limited access to formal education.

In 2017, UNICEF reported that children made up more than 30 per cent of all asylum seekers in Europe; 31,400 of these children were unaccompanied minors. As a consequence of these and other experiences that they undergo in flight and in exile, refugee children are often traumatized and in need of mental and emotional assistance which is not always readily available.

As refugees, children are also exposed to extraordinary dangers such as being forcibly recruited by armed gangs and militias. In conflicts across the world, combatants blatantly disregard international humanitarian law and international human rights law by ruthlessly exploiting child refugees. Children are subject to rape, forced marriages, abduction, and enslavement. Refugee girls are particularly vulnerable. Despite the sexual violence they have been subjected to by soldiers and rebel militias, many girls and young women face discrimination and rejection by their families and communities when they are released from captivity and return home.

Despite all these dangers, refugee children are often characterized by their resilience and their ability to withstand challenges to their physical, mental, and emotional wellbeing. Nevertheless, there is an urgent need for the international community to address the ways that young refugees are managed and protected.

Elderly refugees also face particular challenges. For example, during the mass exodus of Rohingya from Myanmar to Bangladesh in 2017, some of the more striking images of refugees were those of injured or exhausted elderly people who were faithfully carried by younger family members to relative safety in Bangladesh. Mabia, a 75-year-old grandmother whose village was torched, was unable to run and so was carried by her two grandsons in a blanket hung between two bamboo poles on their shoulders. For eighteen days, they struggled through mountainous jungle and across dangerous rivers to neighbouring Bangladesh.

Mabia was lucky. Many older people don't have anyone to help them and are often left behind to fend for themselves. In emergencies, their needs are often overlooked as more immediate needs are dealt with. Older refugees often are frail or disabled and have chronic health problems. Many also require counselling for post-traumatic stress disorder. They frequently need help to find access to food, health and medical assistance, and transportation.

Despite their physical challenges, older refugees also have an important role in their communities. They create a sense of community and participate in local decision-making and camp management. In many traditional societies, older men and women are regarded as wise, experienced people and are generally consulted on important issues. Older refugees are also often perceived as the pillars of community and family life, and many have the knowledge, skill, and ability to hold communities together in difficult times.

An estimated 15 per cent of the world's refugees and other forcibly displaced people are persons with disabilities. For many years,

refugees with disabilities were usually neglected in humanitarian aid programmes.

During my own career as a refugee specialist, I visited dozens of refugee camps and detention centres around the world. Refugees with disabilities in camps were largely invisible and little attention was paid to the problems confronting this group of people. It was only after I became an amputee myself, as a consequence of a terrorist bombing at the UN mission in Baghdad in August 2003, that I became particularly interested in the plight and safety of refugees with disabilities.

In 2005, for example, I visited several Burmese refugee camps along the border between Thailand and Myanmar. I made a point of visiting the few programmes that existed to support refugees with disabilities in these camps to try to understand the conditions under which they lived. In the first camp visited, I set out in my manual wheelchair to find the Handicap International office and discovered that it was located on the top of a rain-soaked and slippery hill. As I looked up, several Burmese refugees appeared on the top of the hill. Some were amputees themselves who had basic wooden hand-made prosthetics as legs. Seeing that I wasn't able to climb the hill myself, they scrambled down and then carried me in my wheelchair up to the office. There they proudly showed me the basic tools they used to make their own and others' prosthetic legs and arms.

While this experience demonstrated for me the resilience and determination of many refugees with disabilities to rebuild their lives, the situation for others is often quite different. In several refugee camps I visited, rehabilitation services were limited and many disabled persons were neglected. Moreover, the layout of these and most other camps made it difficult if not impossible for many refugees with disabilities to access humanitarian programmes and facilities, including those for food distribution, healthcare, and education. In order to improve these conditions, refugees with disabilities need to be involved in planning, assessing, and designing camps and services that more adequately address their needs.

Refugees with disabilities frequently also experience stigmatization and harassment. They suffer physical, emotional, and sexual abuse from their own communities as well as from members of the host country. Similar difficulties and discrimination can also occur after refugees with disabilities have been repatriated to their home countries or resettled abroad. A higher priority needs to be given to the broad range of needs and protection of this group of refugees.

Historically the refugee definition was interpreted through a framework of male experiences and gender bias which meant that the protection claims of many women and persons fearing persecution due to their **gender identity or sexual orientation** have gone unrecognized. Lesbian, gay, bisexual, transgender, and intersexual (LGBTI) persons have experienced numerous instances of homophobic bullying and beatings, persecution, and even murder.

There has, however, been a growing awareness and emerging sensitivity in recent years to the intersections between sexual orientation, gender identity, persecution, and asylum. The challenges confronted by LGBTI communities in their countries of origin, as well as in countries of asylum and resettlement, have started to gain greater recognition. New policies have been designed to promote equality, inclusion, and empowerment both in camp contexts and in the implementation of resettlement and the granting of asylum.

At the same time, however, the widespread discrimination and violence experienced by many LGBTI individuals continues in both countries of origin and asylum and resettlement countries. For example, after taking office in 2016, the Trump administration took steps to roll back protections for transgender Americans by legally invalidating their existence by narrowly defining gender as based on sex assignment at birth. Other countries, particularly in Asia and Africa, have adopted even more discriminatory and dangerous policies against LGBTI persons.

Chapter 6
Civil society, NGOs, and refugees

Civil society is comprised of groups or organizations working in the interest of the community but operating outside of the government and for-profit sectors. Civil society and its partners such as volunteer groups, non-governmental organizations (NGOs), churches and other religious institutions, refugee-led initiatives, and many concerned individuals, families, communities, local and even neighbourhood organizations, women, youth and business societies, academia, and other local groups play key roles in both the Global North and Global South in protecting and assisting refugees. As noted in Chapter 2, offering refuge and protection to forcibly displaced people has been common in kingdoms, churches, and religious institutions throughout human history. Similarly, in recent decades, the efforts of communities around the world have played a critical role in protecting, assisting, and resettling refugees.

Civil society and World Refugee Year (1959-60)

In fact, civil society actors have been drivers of action since the origins of the contemporary refugee system. A number of civil society actors were involved with the drafting of the 1951 Convention, and it was a civil society movement that persuaded states to declare the UN's World Refugee Year sixty years ago. Peter Gatrell has noted that this was the modern era's first and perhaps most successful global social movement aimed at ending protracted refugee situations across Europe, the Middle East, and Asia.

World Refugee Year was inspired by the rapid international response to the 1956 Hungarian refugee crisis, particularly the role played by the voluntary agencies, religious organizations, private foundations, and individual members of transnational society in quickly resettling some 170,000 Hungarian refugees in countries all over the world. Not long after these events, two British journalists, along with the United Nations, and many other civil society groups across the world, spearheaded a unique international campaign, World Refugee Year (WRY) in 1959–60.

The objectives of WRY were to assist a protracted refugee situation and to finally take notice and resolve the plight of the tens of thousands of refugees and displaced persons who remained stuck in refugee camps and settlements throughout Europe, the Middle East, and Asia some fifteen years after their displacement during the Second World War. Ordinary people across the globe were inspired to participate in what became a mass popular campaign against what was described at the time as 'the scandal of the age', in which the international community had abandoned the victims of the Second World War who had not been resettled in other countries and who were still confined to 'DP centres' or similar situations across Europe, the Middle East, and China.

The WRY campaign galvanized public opinion around the world and raised money in order to provide better assistance to and find solutions for the remaining long-standing displaced persons, totalling some 400,000 people. Ninety-seven countries and eighty NGOs participated in the effort, raising approximately $700 million in today's currency value, including almost $100 million contributed by private individuals and associations. In addition to fund-raising and activism on behalf of neglected refugee populations, the WRY campaigned to support broader solutions for protracted refugee situations. One of the major goals of WRY was to raise public awareness about largely neglected refugee populations and to campaign for more liberal and generous policies for refugees and victims of human rights abuses. This was largely accomplished. Politicians and a variety of contemporary celebrities such as Yul Brynner and other film stars publicly supported WRY and appealed for public support for refugees. A refugee camp was set up in Trafalgar Square, London, to demonstrate what life was like for the DPs. The campaign was a huge success. Most of the world's DP crises of that era were finally resolved and all but a few of the DP camps were shut down.

Localized humanitarian action today

Despite the frequent suspicions and hostility directed at refugees and asylum seekers by many people across the world today, compassion and generosity towards refugees and other forced migrants are still alive and well among many societies.

Since the 2015 refugee crisis in Europe, for example, civil society action in the UK has played a crucial role in protecting refugees in transit and on arrival in the UK. Just two examples of this kind of action can be found in the city of Cambridge, where two grassroots, volunteer organizations have emerged in recent years with the goal of supporting refugees. Cambridge Convoy Refugee Action Group has regularly sent food, clothing, and necessary supplies to asylum seekers living rough and stranded in the refugee camps in Calais, Paris, Lesbos, and other 'hot spots' for refugees in France, Greece, and elsewhere in the EU. In fact, one of the defining, yet underreported, responses to the arrival of asylum seekers in Europe in 2015 was the number of citizen responses that were mobilized to help provide assistance and support to asylum seekers.

The second is the Cambridge Refugee Resettlement Campaign (CRRC), one of a growing number of UK-based community sponsorship initiatives. With the support of the national and local authorities, CRRC has been able to sponsor refugees for resettlement and support their integration into the Cambridge community. Members of the group provide food, clothing, accommodation, transport, and educational and social support to newly arriving refugees in the UK. English tuition, social gatherings, and organized friendships help to create networks among both refugees and the Cambridge community. The aim of such activities is to aid integration and intercultural understandings. It was the grassroots initiative of CRRC and similar groups across the UK that finally convinced the UK government to officially launch a Community Sponsorship scheme in 2016, following the lead of countries like Canada that allow community groups to sponsor refugees to be resettled into their communities.

Local activism on behalf of newly arriving refugees in North America and Europe has a long history. Until recently, the United States regularly resettled more refugees than all other countries in the world combined. These efforts were made possible by the active leadership provided by a large number of non-governmental organizations or voluntary agencies (so-called VolAgs). Some of the more well-known ones are the International Rescue Committee (IRC), CARE, Catholic Relief Services, and the Hebrew Immigrant Aid Society (HIAS), but there are hundreds, if not thousands, more organizations working across the country in support of refugees. They all have their own programmes and services and often act as a go-between for refugees and government refugee agencies.

While the United States recently severely cut back on the annual number of refugees it is willing to resettle, other governments have stepped up to try to fill the gaps. For example, for many years Canada has been a leader in refugee resettlement. In addition to the government's official resettlement programme, Canada has had a private sponsorship programme, through which community groups assume the financial and social responsibility of resettling thousands of refugees every year. In 2019 alone, some 19,000 refugees were resettled to Canada through community sponsorship. Several other countries are now following this example and establishing community sponsorship programmes.

Likewise, during times of asylum crises in North America and Europe, churches, synagogues, mosques, and other religious institutions and groups often respond by providing sanctuary for refugees in danger of being forcibly expelled to dangerous situations in their former home countries. This tradition has grown into the emergence of so-called 'sanctuary cities' throughout the United States, the UK, and Europe that actively resist government efforts to deport refugees and migrants.

While there exist many positive instances of organized protection and assistance efforts towards refugees in the Global North, it is mainly the citizens of local communities in the Global South who receive and accept the vast majority of refugees and forced migrants in the world today.

Where there are no national authorities and relevant international actors such as the UN or NGOs, local civil society networks are often the key actors in protecting and assisting refugees from countries like South Sudan, Venezuela, the Democratic Republic of the Congo, Syria, and Palestine. In many contexts where civilians and refugees are at risk from conflict and abuse, displaced people form their own self-protection strategies and actions to shield themselves from repression and forced expulsion.

There are many examples of local citizens' efforts to assist refugees throughout the Global South. For instance, in the absence of a functioning national government in Lebanon, the response to the arrival of more than a million Syrian refugees in that country in recent years was left largely to municipal actors and local organizations. They have been the drivers of some of the most innovative responses to refugees. For example, in Lebanon there are two school shifts in a day—the morning shift for Lebanese students and an afternoon shift for refugee students. This is to ensure that refugees have access to education.

In Uganda, the government has promoted self-reliance for refugees from South Sudan, even in the aftermath of the arrival of 800,000 South Sudanese refugees in 2015–16. Despite the limited response from donor governments to the requests for assistance in Uganda, the government continued to promote an open approach to the resettlement of refugees. There are many reasons for Uganda's generosity to refugees, but civil society has played a large role in making the argument to the national government that the hosting of refugees is good for the country and the national economy.

In West Africa, civil society in Ghana played a significant role in advocating for changes in the recent repatriation of Liberian refugees. The activism by refugees themselves as well as by civil society actors led to important changes that made return more rights based and just. In South Africa, civil society has in recent years promoted anti-xenophobia campaigns to improve the government's stance towards refugees and forced migrants in the country.

International humanitarian action

Alongside those individuals and groups of citizens across the world who play key roles in providing significant humanitarian aid and protection, there currently exist thousands of national and international NGOs which provide assistance to refugees, IDPs, and other people who have been forcibly displaced.

Although traditional hospitality and humanitarian action by civil, religious, and ethnic groups on behalf of refugees and victims of war has a long history in both the Global South and Global North,

Professor Tom Weiss, a leading expert on humanitarian action, has noted that until the late 1980s, there were relatively few international humanitarian NGOs working on refugee issues. For the most part, international organizations like UNHCR and the International Committee of the Red Cross (ICRC) had clear mandates and faced little competition in their work for refugees and for victims of war.

In recent decades, however, there has occurred a virtual explosion in the number and variety of new NGOs who work on refugee issues. During the 1970s and 1980s, regional conflicts sponsored by the two superpowers, the US and the Soviet Union, simultaneously produced large-scale protracted refugee situations in Afghanistan, Indochina, Southern Africa, the Horn of Africa, and in Central America. Both UNHCR and numerous new NGOs worked in highly politicized environments to assist these refugee groups. The militarization of humanitarian aid to these regional conflicts chiefly served the geopolitical interests and aims of the United States and demeaned the principle of humanitarian neutrality promoted by the ICRC and many NGOs.

The size, role, and importance of NGOs focusing on global refugee issues and policies rapidly expanded after the collapse of the former Soviet Union and its client states in the late 1980s. In addition, by the early 1990s, new internal or intrastate conflicts broke out across Africa, Asia, and the Balkans, creating an array of huge new refugee movements and internal displacements. These post-Cold War crises led to a further surge in the numbers of relief organizations, human rights organizations, and NGOs working on international refugee and IDP responses.

At the same time, famines and natural disasters across Africa and other continents gave rise to a number of efforts by both NGOs and civil society celebrities to publicize and advocate for international action and assistance on behalf of victims of famine in Ethiopia and other parts of Africa. These included the efforts of

Bob Geldof's Band Aid concerts, and, more recently, the appointment of UNHCR's Goodwill Ambassadors like Angelina Jolie along with other well-known celebrities to promote the protection of refugees and raise funds for refugee relief efforts.

Not surprisingly, brutal internal wars, ethnic conflicts, and genocides during this period raised questions about the usefulness of international principles that had governed the provision of humanitarian aid since the aftermath of the First World War and which seemed to no longer protect refugees and other victims of war. In particular, confidence in the observance of the principle of humanitarian neutrality was challenged as a consequence of the horrific genocide of Tutsis in Rwanda and the mass murder of Bosnian civilians in Srebrenica in the mid-1990s and the subsequent militarization of humanitarian aid in Kosovo at the end of the 1990s. The terrorist attack on the World Trade Center in New York in 2001 and the growth and expansion of international terrorist groups and organizations during the early 21st century also raised questions about the utility and effectiveness of international laws on armed conflict and future refugee crises.

As a consequence of these events, a proliferation of new humanitarian actors and NGOs emerged to join long-standing organizations like MSF, the IRC, CARE, Oxfam, and others. The newer organizations include thousands of independent international and national humanitarian NGO actors such as Mercy International and Islamic Relief as well as non-traditional actors like the IKEA Foundation. They are now prominent actors and institutions whose activities extend far beyond UNHCR, ICRC, and the UN system.

In addition, many donor governments and institutions now channel their humanitarian aid through their own international, regional, and national bilateral aid agencies, like the US Agency for International Development (USAID), the Department of

International Development (DFID) in the UK, and the European Development Fund in the European Union. This has encouraged a proliferation of NGOs throughout the Global North that compete with each other for funds.

Humanitarian action in a dangerous world

Both refugees and humanitarian actors now face a multitude of new security challenges such as the changing nature of conflict, the worldwide spread of terrorism, and the actions of independent warlords and non-state armed warriors; as well as the growing disrespect for the international principle of humanitarian neutrality and of the rules governing the conduct of war. As a consequence, it has become extremely dangerous for aid workers to carry out their humanitarian work.

In the year 2018 alone, at least 171 aid workers were kidnapped while providing assistance and protection to refugees, another 155 were killed, mostly by warlords and terrorist groups, and 184 were arrested. A growing number of humanitarian workers, both international and local staff, are now at risk of being physically attacked, killed, or kidnapped while providing assistance to refugees and other displaced people. Numerous other international and local national staff suffer trauma and other psychological effects in the stressful and violent contexts in which they work.

Despite a UN Security Council Resolution which calls for the protection of healthcare and medical workers in areas of conflict, doctors and nurses are some of the most targeted civilians in war zones across the world. In some instances the offices of both international and national NGOs in the countries where they work, along with hospitals and schools, have been deliberately targeted, killing or seriously wounding not only doctors, nurses, and aid workers but also patients, including injured women and children and other non-combatants. Humanitarian workers face greater threats to their own safety and security when states remain fragile or failed for a long period. This means there is little prospect for peacebuilding, reconstruction, or repatriation of refugees to their original home countries.

Freedom of the press is also under siege in most conflicts today. The importance of the role of a free press in conflicts and humanitarian action cannot be underestimated. Without reliable information about conflicts and their consequences, humanitarian work would be made even harder. According to Amnesty International, during 2018 more than 50 journalists were killed and more than 250 injured while covering humanitarian crises in ongoing wars. Government-backed groups frequently harass, attack, and shut down independent media and human rights defenders. Journalists in Turkey, Egypt, China, Afghanistan, Saudi Arabia, Myanmar, Brazil, Nicaragua, the Philippines, and elsewhere experience attacks, face threats daily, and are frequently imprisoned for their views and activities. According to the Committee to Protect Journalists, in an attempt to silence the independent media, more than 251 journalists and news photographers were imprisoned during 2018 because of their articles and interviews. Such punishments constitute a direct attack on one of the main pillars of civil society, namely the free press.

Arguably the worst attack ever against humanitarian workers occurred on 19 August 2003 at the UN headquarters in Baghdad when a suicide bomb killed Sergio Vierra de Mello, the UN Head of Mission, and twenty-three staff members. The attack also wounded over a hundred others. Many victims from this and other attacks against NGOs and UN agencies working in refugee situations continue to suffer from their injuries and from the traumatic after-effects of the bombing and violence inflicted upon them. Since 2003 the UN has designated 19 August as World Humanitarian Day to honour those who were killed in the service of humanitarianism and to celebrate the spirit of humanitarian action around the world.

While working in stressful and dangerous situations, those members of civil society who continue to persevere make a huge difference to refugee situations around the world. The hope of a better future for refugees rests heavily with them as well as with refugees themselves.

Refugee-led initiatives

In fact, it is critical to highlight the many examples of refugee communities acting on their own behalf to improve their situations. Refugee-led initiatives in refugee camps like Kakuma in Kenya and those along the Myanmar–Thailand border are actively using new technology in positive ways to offer new perspectives on what refugees themselves think about their situations and what actions should be taken to improve their livelihoods and living conditions. Refugee grassroots media outlets are a promising new factor in global refugee policy, empowering refugee communities through the positive use of new technology as well as the internet, mobile phones, and other means of digital communication.

There are also now dozens of refugee-led initiatives around the world where refugees help other refugees. In June 2018, more than seventy refugee-led initiatives from more than twenty countries gathered in Geneva for the world's first Global Refugee Summit, an outcome of which was the Global Refugee-led Network (GRN), which now advocates for the inclusion of refugees in global refugee policy discussions. Refugee inclusion features prominently in the 2018 Global Compact on Refugees. Refugee inclusion was also an important theme at the Global Refugee Forum in Geneva in December 2019, where more than seventy refugee leaders participated in deliberations and the GRN encouraged states to pledge to enhance refugee participation. The Canadian Delegation to the meeting included—for the first time—a Refugee Adviser as a formal member of its delegation. In June 2020, Canada committed to making this a standing

Refugees

practice and encouraged other governments to include refugees more fully in discussions and deliberations that affect them directly.

The GRN has also worked to highlight the important role refugees and refugee-led initiatives play in delivering protection and assistance to their fellow refugees. In April 2020, for example, the GRN hosted a virtual international conference, involving more than 100 refugee leaders, to discuss the impact of the COVID-19 pandemic on refugees and how refugees have responded. While participants shared the extraordinary impact of the pandemic and state responses on refugees, they also shared how refugee leaders and refugee-led organizations have mobilized to provide support and essential information in response to the pandemic within their regions. In countries around the world, refugees are providing information and training, food distribution, legal support, online mental health support, and transportation for those in need of medical care, and are filling critical gaps in basic services including in health, education, and protection.

These localized responses, by refugees for refugees, are just some of the latest examples of how refugees are typically first responders to crises that affect their communities. The international community needs to do more to understand and support these refugee-led responses in the future. This is especially the case in situations like the COVID-19 pandemic, when international actors, including UN agencies and NGOs, are unable to move freely and access refugee communities.

Amplifying refugee voices

Despite the fact that refugees are often the most authentic source of information about humanitarian emergencies and the best placed to articulate their own needs, they are seldom consulted by government officials, aid workers, and local host communities. This is counter-productive. Such consultations would give refugees a greater degree of ownership and control over their lives and livelihoods and would enable them to make important contributions to their new societies. Greater refugee participation would make policies and programmes more legitimate and effective. The developmental and economic potential of refugees is not often recognized. Building and maintaining the capacity of refugee organizations and local NGOs will help create long-term solutions to the needs of refugees.

Perhaps the most important action international society can take to improve the global response to refugees is to give those who have been forcibly displaced and are in need of protection a voice to express their views and requirements. Governments, international organizations, civil society, and NGOs need to acknowledge that refugees are frequently the best-placed persons to articulate their own needs and to assess the response of the international community to those needs. Yet this does not happen often enough. When the UN General Assembly affirmed the Global Compact on Refugees in 2018, they committed to including refugees in global policy discussions and local programming. It is time to honour this commitment.

Chapter 7
The challenges ahead

In recent years, the international community has frequently failed to provide adequate protection and assistance to many of the millions of people worldwide who have fled their homes in search of safety from persecution or conflict. The passage in September 2016 of the New York Declaration on Refugees and Migration and the subsequent Global Compact on Refugees promised to open new pathways and solutions for refugees. However, the same governments that affirmed the Global Compact continue to fail in addressing the causes of displacement by providing adequate funds, protection, and access to durable solutions for the growing millions of people worldwide who have fled their homes in search of safety.

During the past decade, the number of forcibly displaced people across the world has grown substantially from some 40 million in 1990 to nearly 80 million today. Even with this growth, however, the world's 79.5 million forcibly displaced account for a small fraction of the world's population of 7.8 billion. A solution is surely not beyond our reach.

Given the political nature, size, and complexity of today's refugee problem, no overall permanent solution, or 'quick fix' can be expected. The aim of this concluding chapter is to indicate directions for more effective approaches to refugee situations now and in the future.

Responding to the drivers of displacement

Earlier chapters argued that political and social instability, persecution, and protracted conflicts and refugee situations are on the rise across the world, either as a result of ethnic, inter-community, or religious tensions and conflicts or because of economic and political upheaval in failing states. There is a growing recognition that as long as the increasing scale of forced migration is driven by severe human rights violations, failing states, and intrastate conflicts, the prospect of solutions for refugees depends largely on resolving these contentious issues.

Moreover, as we saw in Chapter 3, while conflicts remain unresolved, not only does the immediate impetus for refugee flight both to neighbouring states and abroad continue but the displaced are unable to return to their home countries. Nearly two-thirds of the world's refugees have been in exile for more than five years and without a solution to their plight. The average duration of a refugee situation is now twenty years. As a consequence, in the long run, the only effective way of dealing with the problem of these protracted refugee situations is to address systematically the conditions that create such problems and to create pathways to solutions.

Arms control is a key factor that needs to be addressed urgently. It is the easy access to and proliferation of arms and other deadly weapons that is generating the majority of refugees and internally displaced persons today. For example, despite the deaths of over 100,000 Yemeni citizens caused by intensive bombardment of civilians by Saudi Arabia and its allies during the past several years, the US, UK, Australia, and other governments and arms manufacturers continue to sell and provide jets, bombs, and munitions to Saudi Arabia and other Gulf states. These arms are used to pulverize Saudi opponents in Yemen, including children and other vulnerable unarmed civilians. If the international community is serious about resolving refugee crises such as in

Yemen, states need to take international action to reduce the availability of arms and to make future aid and investment in countries under siege contingent on the reduction of arms and defence expenditures.

It is also evident that if the international community seeks to curb refugee movements, its efforts should be directed towards creating safer conditions for civilians in countries under attack, such as in Syria, South Sudan, or throughout Central America. Governments and international organizations must take action at an earlier stage of crises to try to influence countries whose internal conflicts might put people to flight and to enable those who have already fled to return home or to obtain a safe solution to their plight.

The largest growth of forced migrants will continue to be internally displaced persons who will be uprooted because of persecution, violence, or environmental change and natural disasters, but who will be compelled to remain displaced within their own countries. Increasing attention will have to be given to the question of how to better provide in-country protection and assistance to internally displaced populations, often in the context of ongoing intrastate conflicts.

The importance of civil society

In response to these growing problems, international organizations need to adopt programmes and policies to involve and strengthen civil society and local institutions in refugee producing and receiving countries. With the growth of these institutions, individual citizens and citizens' groups will be better placed to influence the behaviour of their political leaders through pressure group activities, elections, and other democratic mechanisms. As noted in Chapter 6, advocacy programmes and efforts that promote the cause of refugees, asylum seekers, and internally displaced persons at the local level and the mobilization of public support for these groups have the potential to have a very immediate and positive impact. The strengthening of democratic institutions and civil society are among the major preventive actions against future conflict and displacement.

While promoting the role of civil society, special attention should be paid to the invaluable contributions that refugees themselves can make. Refugee-led initiatives across the Global North and South need to be supported to give refugees an equal voice in the policy process and to help respond to the most immediate needs identified by refugee communities. Many refugee-led initiatives, however, face significant barriers to playing this important role. Local conditions make it difficult, if not impossible, for refugee-led initiatives to gain formal legal status that would enable them to receive core funding. When refugees are given a seat at the decision-making table, they are often required to play a tokenistic role. When refugees organize, they can be seen as challenging the established order of the global refugee regime. Refugees also face barriers in travelling to international meetings on refugee issues in locations such as Geneva and New York, due both to the cost of making such trips and the visa requirements designed to keep refugees out. These barriers need to be urgently addressed if refugees are to play an equal role in developing solutions.

Human rights actors and relief organizations

Recent events in the Great Lakes region of Africa, South Sudan, Syria, the Horn of Africa, and Yemen, among many other countries, indicate that the dynamics of internal armed conflict make emergency assistance and human rights protection inseparable. Human rights NGOs need to establish a continuous presence in regions experiencing conflict and displacement. 'Refugee Watch' organizations should be established within each refugee-producing region to monitor the protection needs of refugees, asylum seekers, and the internally displaced. Creating such organizations could provide a basis for consciousness-raising regarding humanitarian norms and democratic principles within regions, and it could enable local organizations to assume greater responsibility for monitoring, intervening, and managing humanitarian programmes without major external involvement or infringements of concepts of national sovereignty. Such organizations could also provide the accountability that is currently lacking in the global refugee regime.

Relief NGOs, likewise, have an essential protection role to play. Their presence in most civil war situations makes them important sources of information on human rights abuses, quick onset refugee crises and movements, and emergency food and medical needs. This information is crucial for human rights monitoring, early warning of conflicts and refugee and environmental crises, and preventive action and diplomacy. Because NGOs also have a central role in securing humanitarian access to the civilian victims of conflicts and are often in close contact with both governments and opposition movements they can play a significant role in conflict resolution, mediation, and reconciliation. NGOs' presence within communities at war and their ability to move more freely among both civilian populations and armed forces are characteristics not often shared by UN agencies and donor governments. NGOs are well placed to engage in a new comprehensive form of humanitarian action, encompassing assistance and human rights protection, mediation, and conflict resolution.

Post-Cold War humanitarianism has overwhelmingly emphasized the delivery of relief assistance over protecting human rights. Human rights have been perceived as the preserve of human rights NGOs, such as Amnesty International or Human Rights Watch. Apart from the ICRC, however, human rights monitoring and providing protection in armed conflict has often been ignored by many traditional NGOs. Likewise, a number of NGOs involved in relief activities during armed conflicts have regarded many human rights concerns as dangerously political and beyond their mandates. Consequently, in many situations NGO resources and programmes have consistently valued assistance over protection.

Nevertheless, relief NGOs, such as CARE, Oxfam, Save the Children, among thousands of other international, national, and local organizations, have a potential protection role to play. Their presence in most civil war situations makes them important sources of information on human rights abuses, refugee movements, and emergency food and medical needs. This information is crucial for human rights monitoring, early warning of conflicts and refugee crises, and preventive diplomacy. In addition, because some NGOs also have a central role in securing humanitarian access to the civilian victims of conflicts and natural disasters and are often in close contact with both governments and opposition movements they can play a significant role in conflict resolution, mediation, and reconciliation.

Rebuilding war-torn societies

Human rights monitoring and institution-building alone are not enough to create safe conditions in countries of origin for potential and returning refugees. The international community also needs to take adequate account of the relationship between underdevelopment, peacebuilding, and displacement. Relief and development are often still viewed as separate and discrete activities rather than as ends of a continuum. Humanitarian aid activities should be conducted in ways that not only provide relief from life-threatening suffering but also reduce local vulnerability to recurring natural and man-made disasters, enhance indigenous resources and mechanisms, empower local leadership and institutions, reduce dependence on outside assistance, and improve prospects for long-term development. Refugee and relief experts believe that relief and development activities that involve local participation and that benefit both refugees and host communities generally prove more successful than those that do not.

Closer coordination between UN development and refugee agencies is also required in situations involving refugees, returnees, and the internally displaced. Although recently there have been greater efforts at coordination between UNHCR and development and financial institutions like the UNDP and the World Bank, far more effective interagency planning, consultation, and implementation are required. The roles and responsibilities of refugee and development agencies in such efforts continue to be determined on an ad hoc, situation-by-situation basis. In many countries, emergency relief aid is frequently administratively and programmatically divorced from development concerns. Unlike refugee and relief-oriented organizations, development agencies usually work on the basis of long-term plans and programmes, making it difficult to respond to unexpected events such as refugee movements or repatriation programmes. Thus, as Jeff Crisp noted decades ago, a 'development gap' exists between short-term humanitarian relief assistance and long-term development.

UNHCR is not a development agency, and the task of the overall rehabilitation of refugee and displaced communities has to be carried out by UNDP, the World Bank, or by other agencies in the UN system and regional organizations, which can more appropriately deal with reconstruction and development. This requires a transfer of responsibility from UNHCR to the development agencies after the immediate emergency relief phase is over, but this is something which UNDP, in particular, has often resisted in the past because it views itself as having a development, not an emergency, focus.

Rights-based solutions

There is still an urgent need to address the protection of human rights among refugees and other forced migrants. At present, the inclination on the part of many states across the globe to erect new barriers to deter population movements will not make the refugee problem go away, nor will it ensure a stable political base for international relations. Much as states may prefer to focus our attention closer to home, the persistence of refugee problems makes it impossible for the UN and states to ignore conditions that create forced migration. In the longer term, states must recognize that lasting solutions to the problem of displaced people will only be found if a concerted effort is made to defuse ethnic and religious tensions, resolve armed conflicts, protect human rights, strengthen arms control measures, and promote equitable and sustainable development.

In the current international political environment generating support for new international initiatives like these will be difficult. Nevertheless, in the realms of human rights and forced displacement, international and regional stability and idealism often coincide. Policymakers need to build on this coincidence of factors to achieve political will both to address these problems and to develop the institutional capacity to respond more effectively to future refugee crises.

For most of the past seventy years refugee and human rights principles and norms have enjoyed a special status among Western states because they helped define the identity of liberal states. They were also important to non-Western states because adherence to these principles constituted a crucial sign to others of their membership in the international community of law-abiding states.

In recent years, however, many states have viewed refugees and asylum seekers as an unwanted burden and as a security threat. The post-Cold War period has witnessed a declining commitment of many states to the principle of refugee protection and a growing readiness to ignore long-established humanitarian principles. Some governments have seized the central concepts of the new preventive approach to legitimize restrictive measures which oblige displaced people to remain in or return to their homelands or regions of origin and effectively deny people their right to seek and enjoy asylum in another country.

The danger exists, therefore, that a new approach to the refugee problem is emerging among many states in the Global North, based not on the traditional notion of asylum but on the concepts of prevention, containment, and rapid repatriation. An increasing number of governments have closed their borders when confronted with a refugee influx from neighbouring states. The emphasis of post-Cold War humanitarianism has been to pour relief aid into civil wars in order to contain the outpouring of refugees and to stabilize regions. In a number of instances, such actions have been accompanied by the creation of internationally supported safe areas or security zones within the country of origin to which refugees and asylum seekers can be returned. On several recent occasions, states have admitted refugees on a temporary basis while at the same time making clear their determination to repatriate the new arrivals as quickly as possible, sometimes without due regard to established international protection principles, including the refugees' own wishes and the conditions prevailing within their homelands.

In stark contrast, history has shown that the most effective responses to refugees are rights based, comprehensive, and rooted in the principles of protection and international cooperation that are the foundations of the global refugee system. In contexts as diverse as Europe, Indochina, and Central America, these principles have been used to find lasting solutions for millions of refugees. Similar approaches are needed to resolve refugee situations today.

Through shared responsibility, collective action, and the active participation of refugees themselves, solutions are possible. Citizens must demand better from their governments.

Preparing for climate change displacement

Demonstrating the benefits of collective action in responding to displacement will be essential if the world is to effectively respond to the largest and most threatening challenge facing the international community in the coming decades: mass displacement as a result of climate change and natural disasters.

There exists strong scientific evidence and growing international consensus on the impact of climate and environmental change on present and future droughts, famines, desertification, and the loss of habitable land. New conflicts will arise between farmers and nomadic peoples over access to a limited number of pasture lands and water resources that both societies rely on for survival. The frequent occurrences across the world of violent storms and other extreme weather events, as well as the rise of sea levels, coastal erosion, and flooding will create massive internal displacements of people. It will also cause significant new cross-border exoduses of forced migrants.

Since December 2012, the Nansen Initiative, a group of experts and an international consultative process, has advanced legal, policy, and practical solutions for the protection of people displaced by the effects of climate change and natural disasters. Despite the rigorous scientific research and evidence which has been endorsed by 110 states, the international community remains woefully unprepared to respond to the mass displacements that will occur in future years as a consequence of global warming. Some estimates suggest that some 200 million people could be forced across international borders by 2050 if current climate change trends are not slowed or reversed.

This is undoubtedly the most important challenge facing the world today. The international community urgently needs to take steps to more fully address and prepare for these calamities.

Responsibility for the protection of, and assistance to, victims of natural disasters and climate change must be one of the most important areas of concern and activity for the international community.

Conclusion

Displacement has been a defining feature of human history. Over the ages, people have been forced to flee their homes. More than seventy years ago, states created a global refugee system designed to ensure protection for refugees and to find a solution to their plight. Times have changed, but the importance of responding to the needs of refugees remains. While politicians around the world spread fear and suspicion of refugees, we need to remember that refugees are people with rights. Refugees flee their homes out of fear, not by choice. Although the scope and scale of the challenge of refugees seems greater than ever, solutions can be found if states are willing to be part of the solution, if international agreements are upheld, and if the principles of the United Nations—to save future generations from the scourges of war—are finally realized.

Further reading

This book was written to reach a broad readership about an enduring and urgent worldwide political and social issue. There are a vast number of books, journals, and newspaper articles which have been written in recent decades on the subject of refugees. In addition, there are numerous important websites that cover both contemporary and past refugee policies and issues. Here are just a few key texts and websites for further reading on the topics covered in the chapters of this book.

Chapter 1: Who are refugees and other forced migrants?

Alexander Betts, *Survival Migration: Failed Governance and the Crisis of Displacement* (Cornell University Press, 2013)

Elena Fiddian-Qasmiyeh, Gil Loescher, Katy Long, and Nando Sigona, eds, *The Oxford Handbook of Refugees and Forced Migration Studies* (Oxford University Press, 2014)

Guy Goodwin-Gill and Jane McAdam, *The Refugee in International Law*, 3rd edition (Oxford University Press, 2007)

Jane McAdam, *Climate Change, Forced Migration, and International Law* (Oxford University Press, 2012)

UNHCR, *Global Trends* 2019, <https://www.unhcr.org/globaltrends2019/>

Chapter 2: Refugees: a short history

Peter Gatrell, *The Making of the Modern Refugee* (Oxford University Press, 2013)

Gil Loescher, *The UNHCR and World Politics: A Perilous Path* (Oxford University Press, 2001)

Gil Loescher and John Scanlan, *Calculated Kindness: Refugees and America's Half-Open Door* (Simon and Schuster, 1986)

Michael Marrus, *The Unwanted: European Refugees from the First World War through the Cold War* (Oxford University Press, 1985)

Phil Orchard, *A Right to Flee: Refugees, States, and the Construction of International Cooperation* (Cambridge University Press, 2014)

Claudena Skran, *Refugees in Inter-War Europe: The Emergence of a Regime* (Clarendon Press, 1995)

Chapter 3: Causes of refugee movements

Alexander Betts and Gil Loescher, eds, *Refugees in International Relations* (Oxford University Press, 2010)

Kelly Greenhill, *Weapons of Mass Migration: Forced Displacement, Coercion and Foreign Policy* (Cornell University Press, 2010)

Adam Jones, *Genocide: A Comprehensive Introduction*, 3rd edition (Routledge, 2016)

Gil Loescher, *Refugee Movements and International Security*, Adelphi Paper 268 (International Institute for Strategic Studies, 2003)

Gil Loescher, James Milner, Edward Newman, and Gary Troeller, eds, *Protracted Refugee Situations: Political, Security and Human Rights Implications* (UN University Press, 2008)

Aristide Zolberg, Astri Suhrke, and Sergio Aguayo, *Escape from Violence: Conflict and the Refugee Crisis in the Developing World* (Oxford University Press, 1989)

Chapter 4: Responding to refugee movements

Alexander Betts, Gil Loescher, and James Milner, *UNHCR: The Politics and Practice of Refugee Protection*, 2nd edition (Routledge, 2012)

B. S. Chimni, 'From Resettlement to Involuntary Repatriation: Toward a Critical History of Durable Solutions to Refugee Problems', New Issues in Refugee Research, Working Paper no. 2 (UNHCR, 1999)

Katherine Donato and Elizabeth Ferris, *Refugees, Migrants and Global Governance: Negotiating the Global Compacts* (Routledge, 2019)

Gil Loescher, *Beyond Charity: International Cooperation and the Global Refugee Crisis* (Oxford University Press, 1993)

UNHCR, *The State of the World's Refugees: In Search of Solidarity* (Oxford University Press, 2012)

UNHCR, *Global Report 2019* (available online: <https://reporting.unhcr.org/sites/default/files/gr2019/pdf/GR2019_English_Full_lowres.pdf>

Chapter 5: Perceptions and misperceptions about refugees

Matthew Gibney, *The Ethics and Politics of Asylum in Liberal Democracies* (Cambridge University Press, 2004)

Leen d'Haenens, Wilem Joris, and François Heinderyckx, *Images of Immigrants and Refugees in Western Europe: Media Representations, Public Opinion and Refugees' Experiences* (Leuven University Press, 2019)

Susan Forbes Martin, *Refugee Women*, 2nd edition (Lexington Books, 2003)

James Milner, *Refugees, the State, and the Politics of Asylum in Africa* (Palgrave Macmillan, 2009)

Chapter 6: Civil society, NGOs, and refugees

Megan Bradley, James Milner, and Blair Peruniak, eds, *Refugees' Roles in Resolving Displacement and Building Peace: Beyond Beneficiaries* (Georgetown University Press, 2019)

Peter Gatrell, *Free World: The Campaign to Save the World's Refugees: 1956–1963* (Cambridge University Press, 2011)

Peter J. Hoffman and Thomas G. Weiss, *Humanitarianism, War, and Politics: Solferino to Syria and Beyond* (Rowman & Littlefield, 2017)

Kate Pincock, Alexander Betts, and Evan Easton-Calabria, *The Global Governed? Refugees as Providers of Protection and Assistance* (Cambridge University Press, 2020)

Useful websites and journals on refugees and forced migrants

Forced Migration Review:
<www.forcedmigration.org>
UNHCR:
<www.unhcr.org>
Internal Displacement Monitoring Centre:
<www.internal-displacement.org>

Refugee Studies Centre, University of Oxford:
<www.rsc.ox.ac.uk>
The New Humanitarian:
<www.thenewhumanitarian.org>
Refugees Deeply:
<www.newsdeeply.com>
Kaldor Centre for International Refugee Law:
<www.kaldorcentre.unsw.edu.au>
Relief Web:
<www.reliefweb.int>
Refugees International:
<www.refugeesinternational.org>
World Politics Review:
<www.worldpoliticsreview.com>
International Organization for Migration:
<www.iom.int>
Journal of Refugee Studies:
<www.academic.oup.com/jrs>
International Migration Review:
<www.cmsny.org/imr>
Refugee Survey Quarterly:
<www.academic.oup.com/rsq>

Index

For the benefit of digital users, indexed terms that span two pages (e.g., 52–53) may, on occasion, appear on only one of those pages.

Index

CITIZENSHIP
A Very Short Introduction
Richard Bellamy

Interest in citizenship has never been higher. But what does it mean to be a citizen of a modern, complex community? Why is citizenship important? Can we create citizenship, and can we test for it? In this fascinating Very Short Introduction, Richard Bellamy explores the answers to these questions and more in a clear and accessible way. He approaches the subject from a political perspective, to address the complexities behind the major topical issues. Discussing the main models of citizenship, exploring how ideas of citizenship have changed through time from ancient Greece to the present, and examining notions of rights and democracy, he reveals the irreducibly political nature of citizenship today.

> 'Citizenship is a vast subject for a short introduction, but Richard Bellamy has risen to the challenge with aplomb.'
>
> **Mark Garnett, TLS**

GEOPOLITICS
A Very Short Introduction
Klaus Dodds

In certain places such as Iraq or Lebanon, moving a few
feet either side of a territorial boundary can be a matter of life
or death, dramatically highlighting the connections between
place and politics. For a country's location and size as well as
its sovereignty and resources all affect how the people that live
there understand and interact with the wider world. Using
wide-ranging examples, from historical maps to James Bond
films and the rhetoric of political leaders like Churchill and
George W. Bush, this Very Short Introduction shows why,
for a full understanding of contemporary global politics, it is
not just smart - it is essential - to be geopolitical.

'Engrossing study of a complex topic.'

Mick Herron, Geographical.

Human Rights
A Very Short Introduction
Andrew Clapham

An appeal to human rights in the face of injustice can be a heartfelt and morally justified demand for some, while for others it remains merely an empty slogan. Taking an international perspective and focusing on highly topical issues such as torture, arbitrary detention, privacy, health and discrimination, this *Very Short Introduction* will help readers to understand for themselves the controversies and complexities behind this vitally relevant issue. Looking at the philosophical justification for rights, the historical origins of human rights and how they are formed in law, Andrew Clapham explains what our human rights actually are, what they might be, and where the human rights movement is heading.

INTERNATIONAL MIGRATION
A Very Short Introduction
Khalid Koser

Why has international migration become an issue of such intense public and political concern? How closely linked are migrants with terrorist organizations? What factors lie behind the dramatic increase in the number of women migrating? This *Very Short Introduction* examines the phenomenon of international human migration - both legal and illegal. Taking a global look at politics, economics, and globalization, the author presents the human side of topics such as asylum and refugees, human trafficking, migrant smuggling, development, and the international labour force.

www.oup.com/vsi

INTERNATIONAL RELATIONS
A Very Short Introduction
Paul Wilkinson

Of undoubtable relevance today, in a post-9-11 world of growing political tension and unease, this *Very Short Introduction* covers the topics essential to an understanding of modern international relations. Paul Wilkinson explains the theories and the practice that underlies the subject, and investigates issues ranging from foreign policy, arms control, and terrorism, to the environment and world poverty. He examines the role of organizations such as the United Nations and the European Union, as well as the influence of ethnic and religious movements and terrorist groups which also play a role in shaping the way states and governments interact. This up-to-date book is required reading for those seeking a new perspective to help untangle and decipher international events.

www.oup.com/vsi

ONLINE CATALOGUE
A Very Short Introduction

Our online catalogue is designed to make it easy to find your ideal Very Short Introduction. View the entire collection by subject area, watch author videos, read sample chapters, and download reading guides.

SOCIAL MEDIA
Very Short Introduction

Join our community
www.oup.com/vsi

- Join us online at the official Very Short Introductions **Facebook** page.
- Access the thoughts and musings of our authors with our online **blog**.
- Sign up for our monthly **e-newsletter** to receive information on all new titles publishing that month.
- Browse the full range of Very Short Introductions online.
- Read **extracts** from the Introductions for free.
- Visit our library of **Reading Guides**. These guides, written by our expert authors will help you to question again, why you think what you think.
- If you are a teacher or lecturer you can order inspection copies quickly and simply via our website.